虽然我不是富甲天下，
却拥有无数个艳阳天和夏日。

# 向阳而生

## 抚愈心灵的经典英语美文

周成刚／主编

中国出版集团有限公司

世界图书出版公司

北京　广州　上海　西安

# 前
## Preface
# 言

在五彩斑斓的文学世界中，我们会遇见很多让人心动的文字，任凭那些伟人巨匠带我们进入另一个世界。置身其中，如闻其声，如观其行，如见其人，真真假假，虚虚实实。行至深处，甚至能与书中人物一起登台亮相，切身感受现实生活中被我们忽视已久的细节点滴。

诚然，文学的教化作用见仁见智，但真正好的文学作品是能让人产生共鸣的。正所谓"每个人心中都有一座文城"，不管时代如何变化，人生的境遇仍存在诸多相似之处。在这个繁忙的现代社会中，我们比以往任何时候都需要一刻的平静和安宁来抚愈那被城市的喧嚣扰乱的心灵。

本书精选了40篇英语美文，从个人成长、生活选择、人生百态与自然奥妙四个方面娓娓道来，或让人醍醐灌顶，或让人感同身受。这些文字就像阳光，有其魅力和温度，它们能够照亮我们心灵的角落，治愈我们的疲惫和孤独。

在成长的道路上，我们不断地探索、感知和领悟。虽然我们无法选择出身，无法选择父母，无法选择生在哪个时代，但是我们可以选择成为什么样的人：是勇敢无畏还是胆小懦弱，是光明磊落还是卑鄙恶劣，是目标坚定还是随波逐流，这些选择终究是我们自己做出的，无愧于心即可。如果在这个过程中，还能"不因焦虑而迷惘，不因绝望和枯燥而淡漠，不因恐惧而盲目"，那就更好了。

与生活交手，我们开始重新审视日常生活中的美好和幸福。海明威说："智者不会在意他们得不到的东西。"世界瞬息万变，不要把生活当成未来某个日子的彩排，现当下是我们唯一拥有且可以掌控的时间。将注意力放在当下，你就不会感到恐惧和焦虑，因为恐惧是对未来会发生某些事情的担忧，而生活是此时此刻正在上演的瞬间。用心感受此情此景，你会发现：生命的美好其实只与你相隔须臾。它们就在你的身边，在每一刻。

体味人生百态，我们学会思考人生的乐章该如何谱写。林语堂在《人生如诗》中提到：人的一生恰如一首诗，自有其韵律和节奏——无邪的童年、青涩的少年、涉世渐深的壮年、更具容忍之心的中年、内分泌系统活动减少的晚年，直至进入永恒的长眠。这些反复的乐章于生命而言都大同小异，但每个人的乐曲都需要自己去谱写。不是活得热烈的人生才算成功。"大人物经常是千人一面，小人物身上才自带层层矛盾元素"，让人惊喜不断。不然毛姆为什么不愿同一位首相做伴，而是宁愿和一名兽医相守，在荒岛上度过一个月？

最后，不要忘了与自然交流。梭罗曾言："虽然我不是富甲天下，却拥有无数个艳阳天和夏日。"然而，今天的成年人很少有人能真正看见自然，大多数人甚至都看不到太阳，也很少有人能说出今晚月亮何时升起。宇宙的辽阔和大地的广袤我们视而不见，任由数不清的琐碎小事裹挟着我们向前。当生活坚硬的棱角将我们磨得喘不过气时，不妨放慢节奏，重拾我们与自然之间的情感纽带，待白天被理智锁住的那部分思绪尽情奔涌后，内心的平静自会悄然回归。

在人生这场旅行中，我们每个人都在寻找自己的方向。如果中途累了，不妨停下脚步，翻开本书，任意找一篇美文，享受片刻阅读带来的愉悦和满足。无论你是正在经历人生转折的年轻人，还是已经走过半路人生的年长者，都希望你能在阅读本书时从字里行间找到自己，活出一方娱人悦己的小小天地。

# 目

# 窥见自然
## Mother Nature

成长之路

Growing Up

# Man's Youth

Thomas Wolfe

Man's youth is a wonderful thing: it is so full of anguish and of magic and he never comes to know it as it is, until it has gone from him forever. It is the thing he cannot bear to lose, it is the thing whose passing he watches with infinite sorrow and regret, it is the thing whose loss he must lament forever, and it is the thing whose loss he really welcomes with a sad and secret joy, the thing he would never willingly relive again, could it be restored to him by any magic.

Why is this? The reason is that the strange and bitter miracle of life is nowhere else so evident as in our youth. And what is the essence of that strange and bitter miracle of life which we feel so poignant, so unutterable, with such a bitter pain and joy, when we are young? It is this: that being rich, we are so poor; that being mighty, we can yet have nothing; that seeing, breathing, smelling, tasting all around us the impossible wealth and glory of this earth, feeling with an intolerable certitude that the whole structure of the enchanted life—the most fortunate, wealthy, good, and happy life that any man has ever known—is ours—

# 青春

[美] 托马斯·沃尔夫

人的青春奇妙无穷，充满痛楚，充满魔力。年少时不知青春为何物，直至青春一去不复返时才恍然大悟。青春是谁也不忍失去的东西；眼睁睁看着青春流逝，无限的感伤和遗憾涌上心头；青春的流逝是人们心中永远的痛；青春的流逝让人们或大悲或窃喜；即便魔力可以还以青春，人们也不愿再次经历那些流逝的青春岁月。

为什么会这样呢？因为人生中奇特、心酸的奇迹在青春时期体现得最为淋漓尽致。当青春年少的我们怀着或悲或喜的心情，强烈而又不可名状地体味着人生的奇特与辛酸时，我们可曾想过它的本质？那就是：我们富足殷实，却无比贫穷；我们孔武有力，却一无所有；世间的富贵荣华比比皆是，可以看到，闻到，尝到，甚至呼吸到，我们深信不疑，这一整个似乎被施了魔法的生活——人类所知道的最幸运、最富有、最美好、最幸福的生活——是属于我们的，

is ours at once, immediately and forever, the moment that we choose to take a step, or stretch a hand, or say a word—we yet know that we can really keep, hold, take, and possess forever—nothing. All passes; nothing lasts: the moment that we put our hand upon it, it melts away like smoke, is gone forever, and the snake is eating at our heart again; we see then what we are and what our lives must come to.

A young man is so strong, so mad, so certain, and so lost. He has everything and he is able to use nothing. He hurls the great shoulder of his strength forever against phantasmal barriers; he is a wave whose power explodes in lost mid-oceans under timeless skies; he reaches out to grip a fume of painted smoke; he wants all, feels the thirst and power for everything, and finally gets nothing. In the end, he is destroyed by his own strength, devoured by his own hunger, impoverished by his own wealth. Thoughtless of money or the accumulation of material possessions, he is none the less defeated in the end by his own greed; a greed that makes the avarice of King Midas seem paltry by comparison.

只要我们向前迈出一步，伸出一只手，或说上一句话，它便立刻属于我们了，而且将永远属于我们。然而我们也知道，其实我们留不住，抓不着，拿不走，也无法占有什么。一切都转瞬即逝。我们一伸手，它便像云烟般消失不见了。于是，痛苦再一次啃噬我们的心，我们看清了自己，也明白了生活必将归于何处。


　　青年人非常强壮、狂热、笃定，却很容易迷茫。虽然拥有一切，却无用武之地；虽然身强体壮，试图冲破重重虚幻的屏障，却如同一个波浪，最终还是无力地消失在旷远浩渺的大海中央；他伸出双手想要抓住色彩斑斓的云烟，他想得到世间的万物，渴望主宰一切，可到头来却两手空空，一无所获。最终，他被自己的力量打败，被自己的欲望吞噬，被自己的财富弄得内心贫瘠。他对金钱和物质财富的积累不以为意，最后却败给了贪婪，那种贪婪连能够点石成金的弥达斯王见了都觉得自惭形秽。

And that is the reason why, when youth is gone, every man will look back upon that period of his life with infinite sorrow and regret. It is the bitter sorrow and regret of a man who knows that once he had a great talent and wasted it, of a man who knows that once he had a great treasure and got nothing from it, of a man who knows that he had strength enough for everything and never used it.

## 难词释义

poignant ['pɔɪnjənt] *adj.* 令人沉痛的；悲惨的

certitude ['sɜːtɪtjuːd] *n.* 确信；确定

enchanted [ɪn'tʃɑːntɪd] *adj.* 极乐的；施过魔法的

hurl [hɜːl] *v.* 猛扔；用力掷

phantasmal [fæn'tæzməl] *adj.* 幻影的；空想的

devour [dɪ'vaʊə] *v.* 吞噬；毁灭

avarice ['ævərɪs] *n.* （对钱财的）贪婪，贪心

paltry ['pɔːltri] *adj.* 无价值的；无用的

这就是为什么当青春消逝，回首人生的那段时光时，每个人都会感到无限的忧伤和遗憾。曾经杰出的才能，却被白白浪费；曾经殷实的财富，却被挥霍一空；曾经满身的本领，却未能好好利用。一个明白了这些道理的人，回忆起青春岁月，自当会满怀悲痛和懊悔。

托马斯·沃尔夫（Thomas Wolfe，1900—1938）

20 世纪美国文学史上最重要的小说家之一。他创作于大萧条时期的作品描述了美国文化的变化和多样。代表作品有《天使望故乡》《时间与河流》《网与石》等。

# Ambition

## Joseph Epstein

It is not difficult to imagine a world short of ambition. It would probably be a kinder world: without demands, without abrasions, without disappointments. People would have time for reflection. Such work as they did would not be for themselves but for the collectivity. Competition would never enter in; conflict would be eliminated; tension become a thing of the past. The stress of creation would be at an end. Art would no longer be troubling, but purely celebratory in its functions. Longevity would be increased, for fewer people would die of heart attack or stroke caused by tumultuous endeavour. Anxiety would be extinct. Time would stretch on and on, with ambition long departed from the human heart.

Ah, how unrelieved boring life would be!

# 抱负

［美］约瑟夫·爱泼斯坦

一个缺乏抱负的世界是什么样的，这不难想象。或许那将是一个更加友善的世界：没有诉求，没有摩擦，没有失望。人们将有时间进行反思。工作也不再是为了他们自身，而是为了整个集体。世上将不再有竞争，冲突将消失无踪，紧张的生活将成为过眼浮云。创造的重压也将得以终结。艺术不再惹人心烦，其功能将纯粹是用于庆祝。人的寿命将会延长，因世事纷扰引发心脏病或中风导致的死亡人数将越来越少。焦虑将会消失，光阴继续流逝，抱负也早已远离人心。

啊，长此以往，生活将变得多么单调乏味！

There is a strong view that holds that success is a myth, and ambition therefore a sham. Does this mean that success does not really exist? That achievement is at bottom empty? That the efforts of men and women are of no significance alongside the force of movements and events? Now not all success, obviously, is worth esteeming, nor all ambition worth cultivating. Which are and which are not is something one soon enough learns on one's own. But even the most cynical secretly admit that success exists; that achievement counts for a great deal; and that the true myth is that the actions of men and women are useless. To believe otherwise is to take on a point of view that is likely to be deranging. It is, in its implications, to remove all motives for competence, interest in attainment, and regard for posterity.

We do not choose to be born. We do not choose our parents. We do not choose our historical epoch, the country of our birth, or the immediate circumstances of our upbringing. We do not, most of us, choose to die; nor do we choose the time or conditions of our death. But within all this realm of choicelessness, we do choose how we shall live: courageously or in cowardice, honourably or dishonourably, with purpose or in drift. We decide what is important and what is trivial in life. We decide that

有一种很盛行的观点认为，成功纯属谬论，抱负因此亦属虚幻。这是不是说成功实际上并不存在？成就本就是一场空？与诸多活动和事件的力量相比，人们的努力显得微不足道？显然，不是所有的成功都值得景仰，也不是所有的抱负都值得追求。值与不值，人们靠自己很快便能弄清。但就算是最愤世嫉俗的人也暗自承认，成功确实存在，成就举足轻重，把人们的种种努力视为无用功才是真正的无稽之谈。认为努力无用相当于接受了一种可能会造成混乱的观点。这种观点的本意是消除所有提高能力的动机、对成就的兴趣以及对子孙后代的关注。

我们无法选择出生，无法选择父母，无法选择出生的历史时期与国家，也无法选择当下的成长环境。我们中的大多数人无法选择死亡，也无法选择死亡的时间或条件。但是在这诸多无法选择之中，我们确实可以选择如何生活：是勇敢无畏还是胆小怯懦，是光明磊落还是卑鄙恶劣，是目标坚定还是随波逐流。我们可以决定生活中的轻重缓急，决定

what makes us significant is either what we do or what we refuse to do. But no matter how indifferent the universe may be to our choices and decisions, these choices and decisions are ours to make. We decide. We choose. And as we decide and choose, so are our lives formed. In the end, forming our own destiny is what ambition is about.

### 难词释义

abrasion [ə'breɪʒn] *n.* 摩擦；磨损
tumultuous [tjuː'mʌltʃuəs] *adj.* 嘈杂的；动荡的
sham [ʃæm] *n.* 假象；假的东西
esteem [ɪ'stiːm] *v.* 尊重；敬重
derange [dɪ'reɪndʒ] *v.* 使混乱
posterity [pɒ'sterəti] *n.* 后代；后裔

通过选择做什么或拒绝做什么来彰显我们存在的意义。但是无论这个世界如何漠视我们的选择和决定，这些选择和决定终究是我们自己做出的。我们来决定，我们来选择。当我们做出这些决定和选择时，我们的生活也得以成形。而最终，构建我们的命运正是抱负的意义之所在。

约瑟夫·爱泼斯坦（Joseph Epstein，1937—）

　　美国当代知名散文作家、文化批评家，西北大学文学教授，《纽约客》专栏作家。著有《势利：当代美国上流社会解读》、散文集《熟悉的领域——美国生活观察》《似是而非的偏见——美国文学随笔》和短篇小说集《高尔丁的男孩们》等。

# Be Happy

Anonymous

"The days that make us happy make us wise."

—John Masefield

When I first read this line by England's Poet Laureate, it startled me. What did Masefield mean? Without thinking about it much, I had always assumed that the opposite was true. But his sober assurance was arresting. I could not forget it.

Finally, I seemed to grasp his meaning and realised that there was a profound observation. The wisdom that happiness makes possible lies in clear perception, not fogged by anxiety nor dimmed by despair and boredom, and without the blind spots caused by fear.

Active happiness—not mere satisfaction or contentment—often comes suddenly, like an April shower or the unfolding of a bud. Then you discover what kind of wisdom has accompanied it. The grass is greener; bird songs are sweeter; the shortcomings of your friends are more understandable and more forgivable. Happiness is like a pair of eyeglasses correcting your spiritual vision.

# 快乐

佚名

快乐的日子使人睿智。

——约翰·梅斯菲尔德

我第一次读到英国桂冠诗人梅斯菲尔德的这行诗时，感到十分震惊。他想表达的是什么呢？我之前并没有想太多，总觉得这句话应该反过来说才对。但是他文字间透露的冷静与自信俘获了我，令我无法忘怀。

终于，我似乎明白了他想表达什么，意识到这行诗意义深远。快乐带来的睿智存在于敏锐的洞察力中，不因焦虑而迷惘，不因绝望和枯燥而淡漠，不因恐惧而盲目。

积极向上的快乐——并非单纯的满意或知足——通常不期而至，就像四月的春雨说下就下，或是花蕾的突然绽放。然后，你就会发觉伴随着快乐而来的是何种智慧。草地更为青翠，鸟吟更为甜美，朋友的缺点也更容易被理解和包容。快乐就像眼镜，可以矫正你的精神视野。

Nor are the insights of happiness limited to what is near around you. Unhappy, with your thoughts turned in upon your emotional woes, your vision is cut short as though by a wall. Happy, the wall crumbles.

The long vista is there for the seeing. The ground at your feet, the world about you—people, thoughts, emotions, pressures—are now fitted into the larger scene. Everything assumes a fairer proportion. And here is the beginning of wisdom.

### 难词释义

assurance [əˈʃʊərəns] *n.* 保证；自信
arresting [əˈrestɪŋ] *adj.* 引人注意的；很有吸引力的
fog [fɒg] *v.* 使迷惘；使困惑

洞察快乐并不仅限于感受你周围的事物。当你不快乐时，难免会陷入悲伤的情绪中，连带着视野也被这道墙阻隔。但你快乐时，这道墙就会砰然倒塌。

你的视野会变得更为宽广。你脚下的土地，你周围的世界，包括人、思想、情感和压力，在此刻都融进了更为广阔的景象之中。每件事物都变得恰到好处。而这，就是睿智的开始。

# Have Faith in Others

Faith Baldwin

Belief is a happier state of mind than doubt and suspicion.

By this I live, for if I don't have faith in others, who will believe in me? I would rather believe in a thousand people, friends and strangers, and have 999 fail me than not believe. If many fail me, I remember how many I failed. This is not to say that the blind belief of sentimentality, the so-called "tolerance" of the dishonest and vicious, is sensible or rewarding. There are some dark corners which do not react to sweetness and light. Belief in people should be accomplished with open eyes and clarity of judgment. But when your judgment proves bad rather than good, it's no reason to walk thereafter with suspicion as a companion. None knows another's heart, his grief, his struggle, his despair and motivation. Not all our geese become swans, but one swan atones for many flocks of geese.

# 相信别人

[美] 费丝·鲍德温 | 赖世雄 译

相信是一种比怀疑和猜忌更快乐的心态。

我就是本着这一信念做人处事的，因为我若不相信他人，谁又会信任我呢？我宁可信任一千个人，不管是朋友还是陌生人，而且我宁可有九百九十九个人辜负我，也不愿对人不信任。如果众多人辜负我，我会记得自己曾辜负了多少人。这样做并非是说，感情用事的盲目相信，即所谓对不诚实及邪恶的"容忍"是明智或值得的。总有一些黑暗的角落对任何善意与光明都漠然免疫。相信别人应该要擦亮双眼并且有明确的判断力。但是当你的判断被证明是错的而非对的，也没有理由就此便一直心存怀疑。别人的心地好坏、所悲为何、奋斗缘由、绝望原因、有什么动机，我们都无从得知。我们周围的芸芸众生并非个个都能成大器，他们之中只要有一个能成大器就够了。

All men share pain and mortality; some bear these better than others. And multitudes have perished spiritually for the lack of another's belief in them. So, I would rather be disappointed than afraid of disappointment.

難词释义

sentimentality [ˌsentɪmen'tæləti] *n.* 多愁善感
atone [ə'təʊn] *v.* 弥补

所有人都会遭遇痛苦与死亡，只不过有些人的承受力更强罢了。而许多人因为无法获得别人的信任而在精神上形同死亡。因此，我宁可因他人负我而失望也不愿因害怕失望而不信任别人。

**费丝·鲍德温**（Faith Baldwin，1893—1978）

美国作家、演员，20 世纪最成功的作家之一，她的许多作品被改编为电影。

# Man Is Here for the Sake of Other Men

Albert Einstein

Strange is our situation here upon earth. Each of us comes for a short visit, not knowing why, yet sometimes seeming to divine a purpose.

From the standpoint of daily life, however, there is one thing we do know that man is here for the sake of other men—above all for those upon whose smile and well-being our own happiness depends, and also for the countless unknown souls with whose fate we are connected by a bond of sympathy. Many times a day I realise how much my own outer and inner life is built upon the labors of my fellow men, both living and dead, and how earnestly I must exert myself in order to give in return as much as I have received. My peace of mind is often troubled by the depressing sense that I have borrowed too heavily from the work of other men.

# 人是为了他人而活

[美] 阿尔伯特·爱因斯坦

人在这世上的处境真是奇异。每个人都只来这世上短暂地逗留一段时间，不知自己为何而来，然而有时候似乎也能悟出某种目的。

不过，从日常生活的角度来看，有一件事情我们很清楚，那就是人活在世上，是为了他人而活的，尤其是那些我们把自身幸福寄托在其笑容和健康上的人，以及无数由于同情心而使我们与其命运紧密相连的人。每天都有很多次，我察觉到自己的外在生活和精神生活是如何建立在他人——生者和死者皆有——的劳动之上，以及自己必须如何奋发努力，从而回报给别人我从他们那里索取的东西。我时常怀着一种惴惴不安的忧郁心情，觉得自己借用了太多别人的努力成果。

To ponder interminably over the reason for one's own existence or the meaning of life in general seems to me, from an objective point of view, to be sheer folly. And yet everyone holds certain ideals by which he guides his aspiration and his judgment. The ideals which have always shone before me and filled me with the joy of living are goodness, beauty, and truth. To make a goal of comfort and happiness has never appealed to me; a system of ethics built on this basis would be sufficient only for a herd of cattle.

🐦 难词释义 ...........................................................

divine [dɪ'vaɪn] *v.* 猜到；领悟
ponder ['pɒndə(r)] *v.* 沉思；考虑
interminably [ɪn'tɜːmɪnəbli] *adv.* 没完没了地
sheer [ʃɪə(r)] *adj.* 完全的；十足的
folly ['fɒli] *n.* 愚蠢（的行为）

客观来讲，没完没了地沉思自己存在的理由和人生的意义，通常都是近乎愚蠢的行为。但每个人都有自己坚守的理念，以此来指引自己的抱负和判断。始终在我眼前闪耀着光芒，并且使我的生活被快乐填满的理念就是善、美和真理。于我而言，以追求舒适和享乐为目标的生活一向没有什么吸引力。建立在这个基础之上的一套道德规范，只能满足一群动物的需求。

阿尔伯特·爱因斯坦（Albert Einstein，1879—1955）

美国物理学家、科学家、思想家，被美国《时代周刊》评选为 20 世纪的"世纪伟人"。他不仅在科学领域有极高的成就，在哲学（包括科学哲学、社会哲学、人生哲学）思想方面也颇有见地。

# Thirteen Names of Virtues

Benjamin Franklin

I conceived the bold and arduous project of arriving at moral perfection. I wished to live without committing any fault at any time; I would conquer all that either natural inclination, custom, or company might lead me into. As I knew, or thought I knew, what was right or wrong, I did not see why I might not always do the one and avoid the other. But I soon found I had undertaken a task of more difficulty than I had imagined. While my case was employed in guarding against one fault, I was often surprised by another; habit took the advantage of inattention; inclination was sometimes too strong for reason. I concluded, at length, that the mere speculative conviction that it was our interest to be completely virtuous, was not sufficient to prevent our slipping; and that the contrary habits must be broken, and good ones acquired and established, before we can have any dependence on a steady, uniform rectitude of conduct. For this purpose I therefore contrived the following method.

# 十三项美德

[美] 本杰明·富兰克林

　　我设想过一个大胆而艰巨的计划——达到道德上的完美。我希望这一辈子都不犯任何错误，我要克服所有的缺点，不管它们是由天性、习惯还是交友不慎导致的。因为我知道，或者自以为知道，何为对错，所以我觉得自己能够只做对的而不做错的。但不久后我发现，自己想完成的事情比原先料想的要困难得多。当我把注意力放在克服某一个缺点上面时，另一个缺点经常会出其不意地冒出来。习惯会利用一时的疏忽，而理智有时又绝非癖好的敌手。后来，我终于得出结论：仅仅凭臆想坚信完美的品德对我们有利不足以防止我们出现过失；坏习惯必须打破，好习惯必须培养和建立起来，然后我们才能如愿做到举止坚定不移、始终如一地正确。为了这个目标，我想出了下面这个方法。

In the various enumerations of the moral virtues I had met with in my reading, I found the catalogue more or less numerous, as different writers included more or fewer ideas under the same name. Temperance, for example, was by some confined to eating and drinking, while by others it was extended to mean the moderating of every other pleasure, appetite, inclination, or passion, bodily or mental, even to our avarice and ambition. I proposed to myself, for the sake of clearness, to use rather more names, with fewer ideas annexed to each, than a few names with more ideas; and I included under thirteen names of virtues all that at that time occurred to me as necessary or desirable, and annexed to each a short precept, which fully expressed the extent I gave to its meaning.

These names of virtues, with their precepts, were:

1. Temperance. Eat not to dullness; drink not to elevation.

2. Silence. Speak not but what may benefit others or yourself; avoid trifling conversation.

3. Order. Let all your things have their places; let each part of your business have its time.

我在阅读的过程中发现，书中列举各种道德品质时，分类都或多或少地存在分歧，因为对于同一个词的含义，不同的作者可以做或多或少的阐释。例如"节制"这个词，一些人认为节制仅限于吃喝，而另一些人则把它扩展为节制肉体上或精神上的其他情感，包括快乐、欲望、癖好或激情，甚至还将其扩展到贪婪和野心上面。为免疑义，我主张多设条目，每个条目下少包含一些内容，而不是少设条目，每个条目下承载很多内容。因此，我把当时能想到的必要或可取的美德总结成了十三项条目，并在每个条目后面加了一条简短的准则，以充分说明我认为这个条目应包含的意义和范围。

这些美德的条目及其准则如下：

1. 节制。食不过饱，饮不过量。

2. 沉默。只说对人对己有益的话，避免闲聊。

3. 秩序。物归其位，事定有期。

4. Resolution. Resolve to perform what you ought; perform without fail what you resolve.

5. Frugality. Make no expense but to do good to others or yourself; i. e. waste nothing.

6. Industry. Lose no time; be always employed in something useful; cut off all unnecessary actions.

7. Sincerity. Use no hurtful deceit; think innocently and justly, and, if you speak, speak accordingly.

8. Justice. Wrong none by doing injuries, or omitting the benefits that are your duty.

9. Moderation. Avoid extremes; forbear resenting injuries so much as you think they deserve.

10. Cleanliness. Tolerate no uncleanness in body, clothes, or habitation.

11. Tranquility. Be not disturbed at trifles, or at accidents common or unavoidable.

4. 决心。该做的事情一定要做，要做的事情一定做成。

5. 俭朴。花钱必须于人于己有益，换言之，切忌浪费。

6. 勤勉。不要浪费时间，只做有用的事，戒除一切不必要的行为。

7. 诚恳。不要恶意欺骗人，思想纯洁、公正，讲话也是如此。

8. 公正。不做损人不利己的事情。

9. 温和。不走极端，要尽量克制报复心理。

10. 清洁。身体、衣服及住所，力求整洁。

11. 平静。不被琐事、普通或不可避免的事所扰。

12. Chastity. Rarely use venery but for health or offspring, never to dullness, weakness, or the injury of your own or another's peace or reputation.

13. Humility. Imitate Jesus and Socrates.

My intention being to acquire the habitude of all these virtues, I judged it would be well not to distract my attention by attempting the whole at once, but to fix it on one of them at a time; and, when I should be master of that, then to proceed to another, and so on, till I should have gone through the thirteen; and, as the previous acquisition of some might facilitate the acquisition of certain others, I arranged them with that view, as they stand above.

## 难词释义

arduous ['ɑːdʒuəs] *adj.* 艰苦的；艰难的
inattention [ˌɪnə'tenʃn] *n.* 不注意；不经心
rectitude ['rektɪtjuːd] *n.* 公正；正直；诚实
contrive [kən'traɪv] *v.* （不顾困难而）设法做到
enumeration [ɪˌnjuːmə'reɪʃn] *n.* 列举；枚举
temperance ['tempərəns] *n.* 克己；节欲；节食
precept ['priːsept] *n.* （思想、行为的）准则，规范
forbear [fɔː'beə(r)] *v.* 克制；忍住
chastity ['tʃæstəti] *n.* 忠贞；贞洁

12. 贞节。要节欲，除非为了健康或后代。不要纵欲而损伤身体，不要损害自己或他人的安宁与名誉。

13. 谦逊。向耶稣和苏格拉底学习。

我的目标是养成所有这些美德的习惯，所以我认为，为了注意力不被分散，最好还是不要立即全面去尝试，而是在一段时期内集中精力于其中某一项。当我掌握了一项美德之后，接着再开始尝试另外一项，如此这般，直到十三项我都做到了为止。因为先前获得的一些美德可能会有助于其他美德的培养，所以我就按照这个主张把它们排列如上。

本杰明·富兰克林（Benjamin Franklin，1706—1790）

........................................................................

美国政治家、物理学家、作家、发明家，美国大陆会议代表及《独立宣言》起草和签署人之一，美国开国元勋之一。代表作有《穷理查年鉴》《富兰克林自传》等。

# Of Studies

Francis Bacon

Studies serve for delight, for ornament, and for ability. Their chief use for delight, is in privateness and retiring; for ornament, is in discourse; and for ability, is in the judgment and disposition of business. For expert, men can execute, and perhaps judge of particulars, one by one; but the general counsels, and the plots and marshalling of affairs, come best from those that are learned.

To spend too much time in studies is sloth; to use them too much for ornament, is affectation; to make judgment wholly by their rules is the humour of a scholar. They perfect nature, and are perfected by experience: for natural abilities are like natural plants, that need pruning by study; and studies themselves do give forth directions too much at large, except they be bounded in by experience.

Crafty men contemn studies, simple men admire them, and wise men use them; for they teach not their own use; but that is a wisdom without them and above them, won by observation. Read not to contradict and confuse; nor to believe and take for granted; nor to find talk and discourse; but to weigh and consider.

# 论读书

〔英〕弗朗西斯·培根 | 王佐良 译

读书足以怡情，足以傅彩，足以长才。其怡情也，最见于独处幽居之时；其傅彩也，最见于高谈阔论之中；其长才也，最见于处世判事之际。练达之士虽能分别处理细事或一一判别枝节，然纵观统筹、全局策划，则舍好学深思者莫属。

读书费时过多易惰，文采藻饰太盛则矫，全凭条文断事乃学究故态。读书补天然之不足，经验又补读书之不足，盖天生才干犹如自然花草，读书然后知如何修剪移接；而书中所示，如不以经验范之，则又大而无当。

有一技之长者鄙读书，无知者羡读书，唯明智之士用读书，然读书并不以用处告人，用书之智不在书中，而在书外，全凭观察得之。读书时不可存心诘难作者，不可尽信书上所言，亦不可只为寻章摘句，而应推敲细思。

Some books are to be tasted, others to be swallowed, and some few to be chewed and digested; that is, some books are to be read only in parts; others to be read, but not curiously; and some few to be read wholly, and with diligence and attention. Some books also may be read by deputy, and extracts made of them by others; but that would be only in the less important arguments, and the meaner sort of books; else distilled books are, like common distilled waters, flashy things.

Reading maketh a full man; conference a ready man; and writing an exact man. And therefore, if a man write little, he had need have a great memory; if he confer little, he had need have a present wit; and if he read little, he had need have much cunning, to seem to know that he doth not.

Histories make men wise; poets witty; the mathematics subtle; natural philosophy deep; moral grave; logic and rhetoric able to contend. Abeunt studia in mores (Studies pass into the character). Nay there is no stone or impediment in the wit, but may be wrought out by fit studies: like as diseases of the body may have appropriate exercises. Bowling is good for the stone and reins; shooting for the lungs and breast; gentle walking for the stomach; riding for the head; and the like.

书有可浅尝者，有可吞食者，少数则须咀嚼消化。换言之，有只须读其部分者，有只须大体涉猎者，少数则须全读，读时须全神贯注，孜孜不倦。书亦可请人代读，取其所作摘要，但只限题材较次或价值不高者，否则书经提炼犹如水经蒸馏，淡而无味。

读书使人充实，讨论使人机智，笔记使人准确。因此，不常做笔记者须记忆力特强，不常讨论者须天生聪颖，不常读书者须欺世有术，始能无知而显有知。

读史使人明智，读诗使人灵秀，数学使人周密，科学使人深刻，伦理学使人庄重，逻辑修辞之学使人善辩：凡有所学，皆成性格。人之才智但有滞碍，无不可读适当之书使之顺畅，一如身体百病，皆可借相宜之运动除之。滚球利睾肾，射箭利胸肺，慢步利肠胃，骑术利头脑，诸如此类。

So if a man's wit be wandering, let him study the mathematics; for in demonstrations, if his wit be called away never so little, he must begin again. If his wit be not apt to distinguish or find differences, let him study the schoolmen; for they are cymini sectores (Hair-splitters, people who pay too much attention to details). If he be not apt to beat over matters, and to call up one thing to prove and illustrate another, let him study the lawyers' cases. So every defect of the mind may have a special receipt.

🐟 难词释义 ....................................................

marshal ['mɑːʃl] *v.* 安排；组织
sloth [sləʊθ] *n.* 懒散；怠惰
affectation [ˌæfek'teɪʃn] *n.* 做作；装模作样
prune [pruːn] *v.* 修剪；修整
distil [dɪ'stɪl] *v.* 蒸馏；提炼；浓缩
contend [kən'tend] *v.* 争辩；主张
impediment [ɪm'pedɪmənt] *n.* 妨碍；障碍
wrought out=work out 找到（解决办法等）
　　注：在古英语中，wrought 是 work 的过去式和过去分词
reins [reɪnz] *n.* 肾；腰

是以如智力不集中，可令读数学，盖演题须全神贯注，稍有分散即须重演；如不能辨异，可令读经院哲学，盖是辈皆吹毛求疵之人；如不善求同，不善以一物阐证另一物，可令读律师之案卷。如此头脑中凡有缺陷，皆有特药可医。

**弗朗西斯·培根（Francis Bacon，1561—1626）**

英国文艺复兴时期散文家、哲学家。主要著作有《新工具》《亨利七世的治理史》《学术的进展》等。他以哲学家的眼光思考了广泛的人生问题，写出了许多形式短小、风格活泼的随笔小品，本文便是其中之一。

# Universities and Their Function (Excerpts)

Alfred North Whitehead

The justification for a university is that it preserves the connection between knowledge and the zest of life, by uniting the young and the old in the imaginative consideration of learning. The university imparts information, but it imparts it imaginatively. At least, this is the function which it should perform for society. A university which fails in this respect has no reason for existence. This atmosphere of excitement, arising from imaginative consideration, transforms knowledge. A fact is no longer a bare fact: it is invested with all its possibilities. It is no longer a burden on the memory: it is energising as the poet of our dreams, and as the architect of our purposes.

Imagination is not to be divorced from the facts: it is a way of illuminating the facts. It works by drawing the general principles which apply to the facts, as they exist, and then by an intellectual survey of alternative possibilities which are consistent with those principles. It enables men to construct an intellectual vision of a new world, and it preserves the zest of life by the suggestion of satisfying purposes.

# 大学及其功用（节选）

[英] 阿尔弗雷德·诺思·怀特海

大学之所以有理由存在，就在于它联合青年人和老年人共同对学问进行富有想象的研究，从而在知识和探索生命的热情之间架起桥梁。大学传授知识，但它是以富有想象力的方式进行传授的。至少，这是大学应该为社会发挥的作用。一所大学若做不到这一点，那它就毫无存在的理由。充满想象的思考会营造一种兴奋的学习氛围，使知识得以转化——某一事实不再单纯只是事实，而是被赋予了所有潜在的可能。它不再是记忆的累赘，而是充满活力，犹如能描绘我们美梦的诗人和实现我们心愿的设计师。

想象不能脱离事实：它可以让事实变得鲜明生动。想象能如实地提取适用于现存事实的普遍原理，并对符合这些普遍原理的各种可能进行理性的审视。想象能使人们面对一个新世界时建构起一幅理性的愿景，并通过暗示目标有望达成而使人们保持探索生命的热情。

Youth is imaginative, and if the imagination be strengthened by discipline, this energy of imagination can in great measure be preserved through life. The tragedy of the world is that those who are imaginative have but slight experience, and those who are experienced have feeble imaginations. Fools act on imagination without knowledge; pedants act on knowledge without imagination. The task of a university is to weld together imagination and experience.

### 🐬 难词释义

zest [zest] *n.* 热情；狂热
pedant ['pednt] *n.* 书呆子；学究
weld [weld] *v.* 使紧密结合；使连成整体

青年人是富有想象力的，如果这种想象力通过训练得以强化，那他们在很大程度上就能终生拥有这种能力。这个世界的悲剧在于富有想象力的人缺乏经验，而有经验的人又缺乏想象力。愚人无知识，凭想象行事；学究凭知识行事，但没有想象力。大学的任务就是把想象和经验结合起来。

阿尔弗雷德·诺思·怀特海（Alfred North Whitehead，1861—1947）

英国数学家、哲学家。他与罗素合著的《数学基本原理》（3卷）是逻辑研究领域的里程碑。他后期的著作有《关于自然知识原理的探索》和《自然的概念》等，探索了思维与感觉之间的关系。

# The Year of Wandering

Anonymous

Between the preparation and the work, the apprenticeship and the actual dealing with a task or an art, there comes, in the experience of many young men, a period of uncertainty and wandering which is often misunderstood and counted as time wasted, when it is, in fact, a period rich in full and free development.

It is as natural for ardent and courageous youth to wish to know what is in life, what it means, and what it holds for its children, as for a child to reach for and search the things that surround and attract it. Behind every real worker in the world is a real man, and a man has a right to know the conditions under which he must live, and the choices of knowledge, power, and activity which are offered to him. In the education of many men and women, therefore, there comes the year of wandering; the experience of traveling from knowledge to knowledge and from occupation to occupation.

The forces which go to the making of a powerful man can rarely be adjusted and blended without some disturbance of relations and conditions. This disturbance is sometimes injurious,

# 迷惘之年

佚名

从着手准备到投身工作，从学徒到某一项技能或艺术的真正实践，很多年轻人都要经历一段疑惑、徘徊的时期。这段时间常被误认为是浪费生命，但实际上这是一段年轻人可以得到充分自由发展的时期。

对热情、勇敢的年轻人来说，想知道生活是什么，生活意味着什么，生活能给他们带来什么，就好比孩童想伸手去探索身边吸引他的事物一样，这很正常。在这个世界上，每个踏实干活的工作者背后都是一个实实在在的人，每个人都有权了解他得在什么样的条件下生存，他能接触到什么样的知识，他的权力范围有多大以及他能从事什么活动。因此，很多人在接受教育期间都会经历这段踟蹰不前的时期，无论男女。在尝试从这个知识领域转到那个知识领域，从一个岗位跳到另一个岗位时亦然。

将一个人塑造成强者的各种力量，不经过与他人和环境之间的摩擦，是很难被调节整合在一起的。这种摩擦有时可能会带来某种伤害，

because it affects the moral foundations upon which character rests; and for this reason the significance of the experience in its relation to development ought to be sympathetically studied. The birth of the imagination and of the passions, the perception of the richness of life, and the consciousness of the possession of the power to master and use that wealth, create a critical moment in the history of youth—a moment richer in possibilities of all kinds than comes at any later period.

Agitation and ferment of soul are inevitable in that wonderful moment. There are times when agitation is as normal as is self-control at other and less critical times. The year of wandering is not a manifestation of aimlessness, but of aspiration, and that in its ferment and uncertainty youth is often guided to and finally prepared for its task.

### 难词释义

ardent ['ɑːdnt] *adj.* 激情的；热烈的
agitation [ˌædʒɪ'teɪʃn] *n.* 忧虑；烦乱
ferment [fə'ment] *n.* 骚动

因为它会影响人的道德信念，即个性形成的基础。鉴于此，这段经历对后期发展所造成的影响之重要应该得到高度的重视。想象力和激情的萌芽，对丰富人生的感知，以及意识到自己拥有掌控和利用这笔财富的能力，共同造就了这个在整个青年时期最重要的阶段。这一时期拥有的种种可能性是此后任何时期都无法与之相比的。

在这个美好的阶段，精神上的焦虑与骚动不可避免。正如人在生命中没那么重要的阶段能够控制住自己一样，焦虑有些时候也是正常的。踟蹰不前的迷惘之年不代表胸无大志，而恰恰是雄心壮志的表现。年轻人通常也正是在这一时期的骚动不安中明确人生的方向并为人生使命的实现做好最后的准备。

# A Letter of Counsel

George Washington

Newburgh, January 15, 1783.

Dear Bushrod:

You will be surprised, perhaps, at receiving a letter from me; but if the end is answered for which it is written, I shall not think my time misspent. Your father, who seems to entertain a very favorable opinion of your prudence, and I hope you merit it, in one or two of his letters to me speaks of the difficulty he is under to make you remittances. Whether this arises from the scantiness of his funds, or the extensiveness of your demands, is matter of conjecture with me. I hope it is not the latter; because common prudence, and every other consideration, which ought to have weight in a reflecting mind, is opposed to your requiring more than his conveniency, and a regard to his other children will enable him to pay; and because he holds up no idea in his letter, which would support me in the conclusion. Yet when I take a view of the inexperience of youth, the temptations in any vices of cities, and the distresses to which our Virginia gentlemen are driven by an accumulation of taxes and the want of a market, I am almost inclined to ascribe it in part to both. Therefore, as a friend, I give you the following advice.

# 华盛顿总统给侄子的一封忠告信

[美] 乔治·华盛顿 | 周成刚 译

1783 年 1 月 15 日于纽堡

亲爱的布什罗德：

收到我的来信，你也许会感到诧异。但只要达到我此次写信的目的，我想这时间也就没有白费。你父亲似乎对你的节俭赞扬有加，我也希望你受之无愧。可在给我的一两封来信中，他提到了给你汇款的困难。这到底是他手头拮据，还是你需求过大，我只得猜测，但愿不是后者，因为一个懂节俭、明事理的人遇事都会考量再三，会更多想到父亲的处境而不是自己的需求，而且你父亲还要负担其他孩子，不只给你一人汇款；另外，因为你父亲来信中的内容也不支持我的猜测。但考虑到年轻人阅历浅，城里各种罪恶的诱惑诸多，加上苛捐杂税和市场不景气给我们弗吉尼亚人带来的苦难，我几乎认为上述两种猜测兼有可能。因此，作为朋友，我赠你如下忠告：

Let the object, which carried you to Philadelphia, be always before your eyes. Remember that it is not the mere study of the Law, but to become eminent in the profession of it, which is to yield honor and profit. The first was your choice; let the second be your ambition, and that dissipation is incompatible with both; that the company, in which you will improve most, will be least expensive to you; and yet I am not such a stoic as to suppose that you will, or to think it right that you should, always be in company with senators and philosophers; but of the young and juvenile kind let me advise you to be choice. It is easy to make acquaintances, but very difficult to shake them off, however irksome and unprofitable they are found, after we have once committed ourselves to them. The indiscretions and scrapes, which very often they involuntarily lead one into, prove equally distressing and disgraceful. Be courteous to all, but intimate with few; and let those few be well tried before you give them your confidence. True friendship is a plant of slow growth, and must undergo and withstand the shocks of adversity before it is entitled to the appellation.

要始终牢记你去费城的目的，记住你不仅是去攻读法律，还要在专业上出类拔萃，这样才能收获荣誉并让自己受益。前者是你的选择，那不妨让后者成为你的追求。铺张的生活与这两者格格不入，受益良多的朋友往往花钱最少。不过，我并不是一个斯多葛派[1]人士，认为你只能而且只应该和议员及哲学家们为伍，而是奉劝你结交年轻人时要有所选择。结交人容易，但一旦我们与其建立某种关系，再发现他们令人讨厌或一无是处，想要摆脱他们就难了。他们常常不自觉地把人带入鲁莽和尴尬的困境，让人遭受苦痛，蒙受耻辱。对所有人都要以礼相待，但知交则以少为好。即使是知交，也要几经考验方可信任。真挚的友情就如生长缓慢的树木，只有经历了种种磨难，才能无愧于它的美称。

---

1.斯多葛派：古希腊哲学流派，认为智者不应为苦乐所动。

Let your heart feel for the afflictions and distresses of every one, and let your hand give in proportion to your purse; remembering always the estimation of the widow's mite, but that it is not every one who asketh that deserveth charity; all, however, are worthy of the inquiry, or the deserving may suffer.

Do not conceive that fine clothes make fine men any more than fine feathers make fine birds. A plain genteel dress is more admired and obtains more credit than lace and embroidery, in the eyes of the judicious and sensible.

The last thing, which I shall mention, is first in importance; and that is, to avoid gaming. This is a vice which is productive of every possible evil; equally injurious to the morals and health of its votaries. It is the child of avarice, the brother of iniquity, and the father of mischief. It has been the ruin of many worthy families, the loss of many a man's honour, and the cause of suicide. To all those who enter the lists, it is equally fascinating. The successful gamester pushes his good fortune, till it is overtaken by a reverse. The losing gamester, in hopes of retrieving past misfortunes, goes on from bad to worse, till grown desperate he pushed at everything and loses his all. In a word, few gain by this abominable practice (the profit, if any, being diffused), while thousands are injured.

同情每一个人的烦恼和痛苦，并尽力解囊相助。永远牢记：锱铢重千金。不过，也并非所有的乞求者都值得施舍，但无疑都值得我们去过问实情，不然就害苦了那些真正值得救助的人。

不要以为羽毛漂亮的鸟一定是珍禽，也不要认为服饰华丽的人都是好人。在一个有眼光的明智者看来，朴素大方的衣着比堆满绣花蕾丝的锦缎更令人羡慕，受人爱戴。

我要提的最后一点，也是最重要的一点，即切忌赌博。赌博是万恶之源，它不仅败坏赌客的道德，也损害他们的健康。赌博是贪婪之子，邪恶之兄，不幸之父。多少体面的家庭为之倾家荡产，多少英雄豪杰为之名誉扫地，自裁轻生。只要是赌徒，都难以抵抗赌博的诱惑。走运的赌徒总指望一赢再赢，直至时运倒转。倒霉的赌徒总指望挽回败局，结果越输越惨，最终孤注一掷，输个精光。总之，靠此邪道获利者寥寥无几（即便获利，也是挥霍殆尽），而成千上万的人则因此遭殃受害。

Perhaps you will say, "My conduct has anticipated the advice," and "Not one of these cases applies to me." I shall be heartily glad of it. It will add not a little to my happiness, to find those to whom I am so nearly connected pursuing the right walk of life. It will be the sure road to my favor, and those honors and places of profit, which their country can bestow; as merit rarely goes unrewarded.

I am, dear Bushrod,

Your affectionate uncle,

George Washington.

## 难词释义

prudence ['pruːdns] *n.* 谨慎

conjecture [kən'dʒektʃə(r)] *n.* 猜测；推测

want [wɒnt] *n.* 缺少；贫穷

dissipation [ˌdɪsɪ'peɪʃn] *n.* 消散；挥霍

stoic ['stəʊɪk] *n.* 斯多葛派人

irksome ['ɜːksəm] *adj.* 使人烦恼的；令人生气的

indiscretion [ˌɪndɪ'skreʃn] *n.* 不慎的言行；轻率

appellation [ˌæpə'leɪʃn] *n.* 名称；称号

mite [maɪt] *n.* 少量

genteel [dʒen'tiːl] *adj.* 显得彬彬有礼的

votary ['vəʊtəri] *n.* 信徒，崇拜者

iniquity [ɪ'nɪkwəti] *n.* 邪恶

abominable [ə'bɒmɪnəbl] *adj.* 令人憎恶的；极其讨厌的

也许你会说，"我之前的所作所为和你的忠告不谋而合"，"上述恶习都和我无关"。那我由衷地为此感到高兴。目睹我的亲人走在生活的正道上，我倍感欣慰。这无疑是我赞同的生活之路，它必将通向祖国赋予的荣誉和地位，因为美德终将得到回报。

你亲爱的叔叔

乔治·华盛顿

乔治·华盛顿（George Washington，1732—1799）

美国开国元勋之一，出生于美国弗吉尼亚州，美国第一任总统，被称为"美国国父"。

生活剪影
Life Choice

# The Two Roads

John Ruskin

It was New Year's Night. An aged man was standing at a window. He raised his mournful eyes towards the deep blue sky, where the stars were floating like white lilies on the surface of a clear calm lake. Then he cast them on the earth, where few more hopeless people than himself now moved towards their certain goal—the tomb. He had already passed sixty of the stages leading to it, and he had brought from his journey nothing but errors and remorse. Now his health was poor, his mind vacant, his heart sorrowful, and his old age short of comforts.

The days of his youth appeared like dreams before him, and he recalled the serious moment when his father placed him at the entrance of the two roads—one leading to a peaceful, sunny place, covered with flowers, fruits and resounding with soft, sweet songs; the other leading to a deep, dark cave, which was endless, where poison flowed instead of water and where devils and poisonous snakes hissed and crawled.

# 两条道路

[英] 约翰·罗斯金 | 周成刚 译

那是新年之夜。一位老人站在窗前，他抬起忧伤的双眼，朝深蓝的夜空望去。夜空中繁星闪烁，像洁白的百合花漂浮在清澈平静的湖面上。然后，老人又把目光投向大地。此刻，没有什么人比他还绝望。他即将迈向他最终的归宿——坟墓。老人在通向这一终点的路上已经走过六十级台阶，一路上留下的都是过错与悔恨。现在，他身体垮了，精神空虚，心情悲伤，只剩下无人慰藉的风烛残年。

青春的岁月梦境般地浮现在老人眼前。他想起那个庄严的时刻，父亲把他放到两条道路的岔路口，一条路通向宁静、阳光灿烂的大地，那里到处是鲜花、果实，回荡着柔美的歌声，另一条路通向幽深无尽的黑洞，那里毒液代替了流水，魔鬼和毒蛇在嘶嘶蠕动。

He looked towards the sky and cried painfully, "O youth, return! O my father, place me once more at the entrance to life, and I'll choose the better way!" But both his father and the days of his youth had passed away.

He saw the lights flowing away in the darkness, and these were the days of his wasted life; he saw a star fall from the sky and disappeared, and this was the symbol of himself. His remorse, which was like a sharp arrow, struck deeply into his heart. Then he remembered his friends in his childhood, who entered on life together with him. But they had made their way to success and were now honoured and happy on this New Year's Night.

The clock in the high church tower struck and the sound made him remember his parents' early love for him. They had taught him and prayed to God for his good. But he chose the wrong way. With shame and grief he dared no longer look towards that heaven where his father lived. His darkened eyes were full of tears, and with a despairing effort, he burst out a cry: "Come back, my early days! Come back!"

老人又仰望夜空，悲痛地呼喊，"青春啊，回来吧！父亲啊，重新把我放到人生的路口吧，我会选择那条光明的路！"可是，父亲和青春都已逝去。

　　老人看到灯光飘进了黑暗之中，那就是他虚度的年华。他看到一颗星星划过天空，一闪而过，这就是他人生的写照。他的悔恨像利箭，直刺心底。他想起自己儿时的同伴，他们和他一起踏上了人生的道路，可他们选择的是成功之路。在这个新年之夜，他们享受着荣誉和幸福。

　　高挂在教堂塔楼上的钟敲响了，钟声在老人的耳边回响。他想到童年时代父母对他的慈爱和教诲，想起父母为他做的祷告，但是他误入了歧途。无尽的羞愧和悲伤涌上心头，老人不敢再仰望父亲安息的天国，眼泪浸满了他黯淡的双眼，他绝望地大声呼喊："回来吧，我的青春，回来吧！"

And his youth did return, for all this was only a dream, which he had on New Year's Night. He was still young though his faults were real; he had not yet entered the deep, dark cave, and he was still free to walk on the road which leads to the peaceful and sunny land.

Those who still linger on the entrance of life, hesitating to choose the right road, remember that when years are passed and your feet stumble on the dark mountains, you will cry bitterly, but in vain: "O youth, return! Oh give me back my early days!"

🐟 难词释义 ......................................................... •

remorse [rɪ'mɔːs] *n.* 懊悔；自责
resound [rɪ'zaʊnd] *v.* 回响；回荡
stumble ['stʌmbl] *v.* 绊脚；跌跌撞撞地走

他的青春真的回来了，因为这一切只是他在新年之夜做的一场梦。他还年轻，尽管犯下的错误是真的，但他还没有坠入那黑暗的深渊。他仍能自由地踏上光明的人生之路，走向硕果摇曳的和煦大地。

仍在人生路口徘徊，不知选择哪条道路的人们啊，请记住：当岁月流逝，你在黑暗的群山中蹒跚独行时，你会绝望又徒劳地呼喊，"青春啊，回来吧！请把我的青春年华还给我吧！"

约翰·罗斯金（John Ruskin，1819—1900）

19世纪英国杰出的作家、艺术家、评论家。著有《时至今日》《芝麻与百合》《劳动者的力量》等，其作品对后世影响深远。

# The Man and the Opportunity

Orison Marden

The lack of opportunity is ever the excuse of a weak, vacillating mind. Opportunities! Every life is full of them.

Every lesson in school or college is an opportunity. Every examination is a chance in life. Every business transaction is an opportunity—an opportunity to be polite, an opportunity to be manly, an opportunity to be honest, an opportunity to make friends. Every proof of confidence in you is a great opportunity. Every responsibility thrust upon your strength and your honour is priceless. Existence is the privilege of effort, and when that privilege is met like a man, opportunities to succeed along the line of your aptitude will come faster than you can use them.

Young men and women, why do you stand here all the day idle? Was the land all occupied before you were born? Has the earth ceased to yield its increase? Are the seats all taken? The positions all filled? The chances all gone? Are the resources of your country fully developed? Are the secrets of nature all mastered? Is there no way in which you can utilise these passing moments to improve yourself or benefit another?

# 人与机遇

［美］奥里森·马登

意志薄弱、优柔寡断的人总是把缺乏机会作为借口。机遇！在每个人的生活中都无处不在！

学校里的每一堂课都是一次机遇。每一场考试都是人生的一次契机。每一次商务往来都是一次机会——一次礼貌待人的机会，一次果敢行事的机会，一次诚实守信的机会，一次广交朋友的机会。每一份他人对你的信任都是一个莫大的机会。基于你的才干和荣誉而寄予你的每一份责任都是无价的。生存是奋斗赋予的特权，当你如勇者般通过努力邂逅那份殊荣时，一个个助你获得成功的机会便会接踵而至，令你应接不暇。

年轻的小伙子和姑娘们啊，为何你们整日踯躅不前，虚度光阴？难道在你们出生之前，每一寸土地都已为他人所占？难道地球已不再繁衍生息？难道所有席位都已占满？难道所有职位都已人满为患？难道所有机会都一去不返？难道你们国家的资源都已开发殆尽？难道大自然的奥秘都已完全通晓？难道你们无法抓住这些转瞬即逝的时机来提高自我或造福他人？

Don't wait for your opportunity. Make it, make it as Napoleon made his in a hundred "impossible" situations. Make it, as all leaders of men, in war and in peace, have made their chances of success. Make it, as every man must, who would accomplish anything worth the effort. Golden opportunities are nothing to laziness, but industry makes the commonest chances golden.

难词释义 ......

vacillate ['væsəleɪt] *v.* 犹豫，踌躇
transaction [træn'zækʃn] *n.* 交易，业务

切莫株守机遇。去创造机遇，正如拿破仑在无数次"绝"境中创造逢生的机会那样。去创造机遇，正如战争与和平年代的领袖们创造他们取得成功的机遇那样。去创造机遇，任何付出努力想要有所收获的人都必须这么做。对懒汉来说，即使天赐良机，也会化为乌有，但勤奋却能让最微小的机遇变得灿烂辉煌！

奥里森·马登（Orison Marden，1848—1924）

美国成功学的奠基人，影响世界的励志导师之一。他的著作有一种不可思议的魅力，通过其积极的生活哲学，激励和鼓舞了无数年轻人奋发向上、不断改变自我，以获取幸福的人生。

# On Achieving Success

Ernest Hemingway

We cannot travel every path. Success must be won along one line. We must make our business the one life purpose to which every other must be subordinate.

I hate a thing done by halves. If it be right, do it boldly. If it be wrong, leave it undone.

The men of history were not perpetually looking into the mirror to make sure of their own size. Absorbed in their work they did it. They did it so well that the wondering world sees them to be great, and labeled them accordingly.

To live with a high ideal is a successful life. It is not what one does, but what one tries to do, that makes a man strong. "Eternal vigilance," it has been said, "is the price of liberty." With equal truth it may be said, "Unceasing effort is the price of success."

If we do not work with our might, others will; and they will outstrip us in the race, and pluck the prize from our grasp.

Success grows less and less dependent on luck and chance. Self-distrust is the cause of most of our failures.

# 论获得成功

[美] 欧内斯特·海明威

我们无法将每条路都走一遍。要想获得成功就必须坚守一条道路。我们必须给自己设定一个终生目标，在它面前，其他目标都得靠后。

我讨厌做事半途而废。如果这件事是正确的，就大胆去做。如果这件事是错误的，那就及时止损。

历史长河中的伟人并非终日对镜衡量自身形象，而是全身心地投入自己所从事的事业。他们是如此的超尘拔俗，是以大众觉得他们很伟大，于是称之为伟人。

拥有崇高理想的人生才是成功的人生。使人变强大的，不是这个人做了什么，而是他努力去做什么。有人说过，"自由的代价是永恒的警惕"，那同样也可以说，"成功的代价是不懈的努力"。

如果我们不拼尽全力，总有人会，随后他们会在竞争中超过我们，从我们手中夺走殊荣。

成功越来越不靠运气和机遇。自我怀疑是导致我们失败的主因。

The great and indispensable help to success is character. Character is a crystallized habit, the result of training and conviction. Every character is influenced by heredity, environment and education. But these apart, if every man were not to be a great extent the architect of his own character, he would be a fatalist, and irresponsible creature of circumstances.

Instead of saying that man is a creature of circumstance, it would be nearer the mark to say that man is the architect of circumstance. From the same materials one man builds palaces, another hovel. Bricks and mortar are mortar and bricks, until the architect can make them something else.

The true way to gain much is never to desire to gain too much. Wise men don't care for what they can't have.

### 难词释义

vigilance ['vɪdʒɪləns] *n.* 警觉；警惕
outstrip [ˌaʊt'strɪp] *v.* 超过；胜过
heredity [hə'redəti] *n.* 遗传

性格是获得成功最不可或缺的一部分。它是一种固化的习惯，是不断练习且信念坚定的结果。每种性格都会受遗传因素、环境和教育的影响。但除此之外，如果一个人在很大程度上不能成为自身性格的构筑者，那么他就会成为宿命论者，成为环境里的无用造物。

与其说人是环境的造物，不如说人是环境的建筑师更加贴切。用同样的材料，有人能建成宫殿，有人却只能堆出简陋的小屋。砖泥只是砖泥，是建筑师将它们变成了了不起的东西。

想得到的多，就不要奢望得到太多。智者不会在意他们得不到的东西。

欧内斯特·海明威（Ernest Hemingway，1899—1961）

美国作家、记者，1954年获得诺贝尔文学奖，被认为是20世纪最著名的小说家之一，因其笔锋冷峻犀利而以"文坛硬汉"著称。代表作有《老人与海》《太阳照常升起》《永别了，武器》等。

# Work and Pleasure

## Winston Churchill

To be really happy and really safe, one ought to have at least two or three hobbies, and they must all be real. It is no use starting late in life to say: "I will take an interest in this or that." Such an attempt only aggravates the strain of mental effort. A man may acquire great knowledge of topics unconnected with his daily work, and yet hardly get any benefit or relief. It is no use doing what you like; you have got to like what you do. Broadly speaking, human beings may be divided into three classes: those who are toiled to death, those who are worried to death, and those who are bored to death. It is no use offering the manual laborer, tired out with a hard week's sweat and effort, the chance of playing a game of football or baseball on Saturday afternoon. It is no use inviting the politician or the professional or business man, who has been working or worrying about serious things for six days, to work or worry about trifling things at the weekend.

# 工作和娱乐

[英] 温斯顿·丘吉尔

要想获得真正的快乐与安宁，一个人至少应该有两三种爱好，而且必须是真正的爱好。在晚年的时候才说"我要培养这个或那个爱好"已经毫无意义。这种尝试只会加重精神负担。一个人可以获得与自己日常工作无关的广博知识，但很难有收益或倍感放松。做喜欢的事没有什么用，你要喜欢自己所做的事。从广义上来说，人可以分为三类：过劳致死之人，忧虑致死之人和无聊致死之人。对于那些体力劳动者来说，一周的汗水与辛劳已经让他们筋疲力尽，所以为他们提供星期六下午踢足球或打棒球的机会毫无意义。对于那些政治家、专业人士或商业人士来说，在为一些重要的事情操劳了六天后，让他们在周末再为一些琐碎之事劳烦伤神也是毫无意义。

It may also be said that rational, industrious, useful human beings are divided into two classes: first, those whose work is work and whose pleasure is pleasure; and secondly, those whose work and pleasure are one. Of these the former are the majority. They have their compensations. The long hours in the office or the factory bring with them as their reward, not only the means of sustenance, but a keen appetite for pleasure even in its simplest and most modest forms. But fortune's favoured children belong to the second class. Their life is a natural harmony. For them the working hours are never long enough. Each day is a holiday, and ordinary holidays when they come are grudged as enforced interruptions in an absorbing vacation. Yet to both classes the need of an alternative outlook, of a change of atmosphere, of a diversion of effort, is essential. Indeed, it may well be that those whose work is their pleasure are those who most need the means of banishing it at intervals from their minds.

🐬 难词释义

aggravate ['ægrəveɪt] *v.* 使严重；使恶化
toil [tɔɪl] *v.* （长时间）苦干，辛勤劳作
trifling ['traɪflɪŋ] *adj.* 琐碎的；微不足道的
sustenance ['sʌstənəns] *n.* 生计；营养；食物
grudge [grʌdʒ] *v.* 嫌恶
banish ['bænɪʃ] *v.* 摆脱；驱逐

也可以这样说，理智、勤奋、有用的人可以分为两类：对第一类人而言，工作是工作，娱乐是娱乐；对第二类人而言，工作就是娱乐。其中，第一类人占绝大多数。他们得到了相应的补偿。在办公室或工厂长时间的工作，带给他们的不仅是维持生计的薪酬，还有对娱乐的强烈渴望，即便这种娱乐很简单、很普通。但第二类人才是命运眷顾之人。他们的生活自然而和谐。对他们来说，工作时间永远不够长，每一天都是假期。当正常的假期到来时，他们反倒会抱怨自己正享受其中的假期被强行打断。然而，有些事情对这两类人来说是同样至关重要的，那就是转换一下视角，改变一下氛围，尝试一些不同的事物。事实上，那些把工作视为娱乐的人最应该时不时地通过某种方式将工作赶出大脑。

温斯顿·丘吉尔（Winston Churchill，1874—1965）

英国政治家、历史学家、画家、演说家、作家，曾两度出任英国首相。

# Change Makes Life Beautiful

Walter Pater

To regard all things and principles of things as inconstant modes or fashions has more and more become the tendency of modern thought. Let us begin with that which is without—our physical life. Fix upon it in one of its more exquisite intervals, the moment, for instance, of delicious recoil from the flood of water in summer heat.

What is the whole physical life in that moment but a combination of natural elements to which science gives their names? But these elements, phosphorus and lime and delicate fibres, are present not in the human body alone: we detect them in places most remote from it. Our physical life is a perpetual motion of them—the passage of the blood, the wasting and repairing of the lenses of the eye, the modification of the tissues of the brain under every ray of light and sound—processes which science reduces to simpler and more elementary forces.

# 生命因变化而美丽

[英] 沃尔特·佩特

视一切事物及其原则为不断变化的模式或风尚已日益成为当代思潮发展的趋势。我们先从外部的事情——我们的生理活动——说起。选取一个无比微妙的间隙，譬如，在炎炎酷暑中猛然浸入滔滔清流那一刹那极度愉悦的冲击感。

在那一刻，一切生理活动难道不是被科学赋予名称的各种自然元素的化合作用吗？但是这些元素，比如磷、钙和微细的纤维，并不仅仅存在于人体之中：在与人体毫不相关的地方也能发现它们。我们的生理活动就是这些元素的恒久运动——如血液的流动，眼睛晶状体的受损与修复，每一束光线、每一段声波给脑组织带来的变化——这些过程都被科学还原为更简单、更基本的力量的作用。

Like the elements of which we are composed, the action of these forces extends beyond us: it rusts iron and ripens corn. Far out on every side of us those elements are broadcast, driven in many currents; and birth and gesture and death and the springing of violets from the grave are but a few out of ten thousand resultant combinations.

That clear, perpetual outline of face and limb is but an image of ours, under which we group them a design in a web, the actual threads of which pass out beyond it. This at least of flame—like our life has, that it is but the concurrence, renewed from moment to moment, of forces parting sooner or later on their ways.

🐟 难词释义

recoil [rɪˈkɔɪl] *n.* 反冲；后坐力
phosphorus [ˈfɒsfərəs] *n.* 磷
perpetual [pəˈpetʃuəl] *adj.* 不间断的；长久的
concurrence [kənˈkʌrəns] *n.* 同时发生；同时出现

正如人的身体所赖以构成的元素一样，这些力量在人体之外也同样发挥着作用：使铁生锈，使谷物成熟。那些元素在各种流动力的作用下，在人体外向四面八方传播：诞生、姿态、死亡以及坟头上紫罗兰的绽放，皆不过是成千上万种元素化合作用结果中的零光片羽而已。

人类轮廓分明，面容恒久，不过是一种表象。在这种表象之下，各种元素被组合在一起，织成网状，其中的丝线则穿过这张网向外延展，又引向他方。在这一点上，我们的生命有些像那火焰，它是各种力量的汇集，虽不断重生延续，但迟早会飘散。

沃尔特·佩特（Walter Pater，1839—1894）

英国著名文艺批评家、作家，提倡"为艺术而艺术"，文风精练、准确且华丽，其散文和理论在英国文学发展的历程中有着很高的地位。

# How to Spend a Day

Anonymous

Do you feel overwhelmed and tired? Is there not enough time in the day for you? Maybe it's time to step back and take a look at what is really important in your life.

Sometimes ignorance can be bliss. Don't get me wrong. I'm not talking about being uneducated or stupid. Learn and read, watch the news once, twice a day. However, do you really need to have a news programme streaming in the background twenty four hours a day? Do you need screen in screen on your television? What I am saying is, do we have to know everything all the time? When is too much knowledge too much? Can a person have too much useless information? Do we need to know all about the Octomom's new house, or exactly what is going on with Michael Jackson's doctors?

Can you remember when there were no computers, no cellphones or laptops? A simpler time. When a friend called you and you were not home, if they really wanted to talk to you, if it was urgent, they called back. No big deal. Or maybe you

# 如何度过每一天

佚名

你是否感到不知所措，疲惫不堪？好像时间总也不够用？或许是时候退后一步，想想你的生活中最重要的是什么了。

有时候，无知也是一种福气。别误会！我说的不是没文化或者愚蠢。学习，读书，看新闻，一天一次或两次。但是，你真的需要一天24小时播放新闻节目作为背景音吗？你有必要让电视屏幕通过画中画窗口播放吗？我是说，我们真的有必要时刻知道所有的事情吗？什么时候太多的知识会显得太多？一个人能背负太多无用的信息吗？我们有必要知道八胞胎妈妈的新房子长什么样吗？或者有必要知道迈克尔·杰克逊的医生到底怎么了吗？

你还记得以前没有电脑、没有手机、没有笔记本的时候吗？那个时代更加简单。朋友打电话给你，但你不在家，如果他们真的有话要和你说，或者事出紧急，他们会再打电话过来。没什么大不了的。或者你

had an answering machine. The friend would leave a message. And when you had time, you would call them back. Sounds simple right? Kind of nice.

Now, however there is no time to take. Because when you are on the phone talking or texting, bleep, bleep, call waiting comes on telling you there is someone waiting for you, so you put the person you are talking to on hold and talk to the person that was waiting. Now someone else is waiting for you and your precious time. Probably you have a cellphone, and it's ringing too. If you don't answer these calls, they go to voice mail and you will have a million messages to sift through. Messages that you listen to, or save, or delete. This takes up more of your valuable time. Ask yourself this: Do I need all this stuff? Do I need to be available twenty four hours a day? I am not the president! I cannot think of one reason outside of a medical emergency why anyone would need to be available during day to day life. If it's not an emergency, call me back. Now when people call a phone and get a busy signal, they get mad. They get an attitude like it's not fair or something.

有电话答录机，朋友会给你留言，等你有时间的时候再给他们回电。听起来很简单，对吧？也是非常好的生活模式。

但是现在，没有那么多闲暇时间了。因为你总是在不停地打电话或发短信，"嘀嘀——嘀嘀——"，呼叫等待告诉你有人在给你打电话，所以你让正在和你通话的那个人稍等一下，然后接通那个正打来的电话。如此一来，另外一个人又在等你拨冗和他继续通话了。也许你还有一个手机，它也响了。如果你不接听这些电话，它们就会转到你的语音信箱，然后你就会有上百万条的信息需要查听。你查听这些信息，选择保存或者删除它们，这些都占据了你很多宝贵的时间。问问你自己，我真的需要这些吗？我真的需要每天 24 小时随叫随到吗？我又不是总统！除了医疗紧急情况之外，我想不出还有什么能让人们每天在日常生活中随时待命。如果不是紧急情况，再打过来又何妨？现在，人们打电话时如果听到的是忙音，就会抓狂。他们会觉得这不公平之类的。

There are hundreds and hundreds of social networking sites on the Internet. Sites where people post all the details of their lives. So other people can do what exactly? I'm not sure, but we have this need to know. I believe I do not have to know everything about everybody. I would like to keep some things a mystery.

So we should just stop. Stop texting, typing, calling, and emailing and spend some time with our families and friends. In person, face to face. Go for a walk. Get some kind of exercise. Kind of like the WII system, only with real people and fresh air. Maybe the less information we stuff into our brains, the more time we will have for our lives.

难词释义

overwhelmed [ˌəʊvə'welmd] *adj.* 被压倒的；不知所措的
bliss [blɪs] *n.* 极乐
stream [striːm] *v.* 用流式传播收听（收看）
sift through 细查，详查

互联网上有成千上万个社交网站。人们把生活的点点滴滴都发布在网上，以便其他人可以依葫芦画瓢地照着做吗？我不太清楚，但我们有必要知道：不是非得了解每个人的每一件事。我情愿给有些事情留点神秘感。

所以我们应该停下来。停止发短信，停止打字，停止打电话，停止发电子邮件，多花点时间和家人、朋友待在一起，和他们面对面地交流。去散散步，做做运动。有点像在 WII 系统里，与真人相处，尽情呼吸新鲜的空气。也许我们往脑子里少塞点东西，就会有更多的时间来享受生活。

# Three Passions I Have Lived For

Bertrand Russell

Three passions, simple but overwhelmingly strong, have governed my life: the longing for love, the search for knowledge, and unbearable pity for the suffering of mankind. These passions, like great winds, have blown me hither and thither, in a wayward course over a deep ocean of anguish, reaching to the very verge of despair.

I have sought love, first, because it brings ecstasy—ecstasy so great that I would often have sacrificed all the rest of my life for a few hours for this joy. I have sought it, next, because it relieves loneliness—that terrible loneliness in which one shivering consciousness looks over the rim of the world into the cold unfathomable lifeless abyss. I have sought it, finally, because in the union of love I have seen, in a mystic miniature, the prefiguring vision of the heaven that saints and poets have imagined. This is what I sought, and though it might seem too good for human life, this is what—at last—I have found.

# 我为之而活的三种激情

[英] 伯特兰·罗素 | 秦云 译

三种单纯而极其强烈的激情支配着我的一生，那就是对爱情的渴望、对知识的追求，以及对人类苦难的深切同情。这些激情犹如狂风，把我吹到痛苦的深海上空东抛西掷，直达绝望的边缘。

我追求爱情，首先是因为它叫我销魂。爱情令人销魂的魅力使我常常甘愿牺牲余生来换取几小时这样的快乐。我追求爱情，其次是因为它能减轻孤寂——那种心灵在战栗，仿若站在世界边缘望着冰冷、死寂的无底深渊时所感到的可怕的孤独。我追求爱情，还因为在爱的交融中，我看到了圣贤和诗人所想象的天堂的神秘缩影。这就是我所追求的，尽管对人生来说似乎过于美好，但我最终还是找到了它。

With equal passion I have sought knowledge. I have wished to understand the hearts of men. I have wished to know why the stars shine... A little of this, but not much, I have achieved.

Love and knowledge, so far as they were possible, led upward toward the heavens. But always pity brought me back to earth. Echoes of cries of pain reverberate in my heart. Children in famine, victims tortured by oppressors, helpless old people a hated burden to their sons, and the whole world of loneliness, poverty, and pain make a mockery of what human life should be. I long to alleviate the evil, but I cannot, and I too suffer.

This has been my life. I have found it worth living, and would gladly live it again if the chance were offered me.

🐬 难词释义

wayward ['weɪwəd] *adj.* 难以控制的；任性的
ecstasy ['ekstəsi] *n.* 狂喜；陶醉；入迷
unfathomable [ʌn'fæðəməbl] *adj.* 莫测高深的
prefigure [ˌpriː'fɪgə] *v.* 预示；预兆
reverberate [rɪ'vɜːbəreɪt] *v.* 回响；回荡

我以同样的热情追求知识。我渴望理解人心；我想了解星辰为何闪亮……在这些方面我略有成就，但不多。

爱情和知识尽可能地把我向上引往天堂，但是同情又总把我带回尘世。痛苦的喊叫声在我心中回荡。饥饿的孩子，被压迫者折磨的受害者，被子女视为可憎负担的无助老人，以及全世界触目皆是的孤独、贫困和痛苦——这些都是对人类生活理想的嘲弄。我渴望能减轻恶，但我无能为力，于是也身处痛苦之中。

这就是我的一生。我觉得这一生是值得活的。如果再给我一次机会，我将欣然再活一次。

伯特兰·罗素（Bertrand Russell，1872—1970）

英国哲学家、数学家、逻辑学家、历史学家和文学家。主要作品有《西方哲学史》《哲学问题》《心的分析》《物的分析》等。罗素的散文在英国文学中享誉甚高，本文是其中广为阅读的一篇。

# Nobel Prize Acceptance Speech

### William Faulkner

I feel that this award was not made to me as a man, but to my work—a life's work in the agony and sweat of the human spirit, not for glory and least of all for profit, but to create out of the materials of the human spirit something which did not exist before. So this award is only mine in trust. It will not be difficult to find a dedication for the money part of it commensurate with the purpose and significance of its origin. But I would like to do the same with the acclaim too, by using this moment as a pinnacle from which I might be listened to by the young men and women already dedicated to the same anguish and travail, among whom is already that one who will some day stand here where I am standing.

Our tragedy today is a general and universal physical fear so long sustained by now that we can even bear it. There are no longer problems of the spirit. There is only the question: When will I be blown up? Because of this, the young man or woman writing today has forgotten the problems of the human heart in conflict with itself which alone can make good writing because only that is worth writing about, worth the agony and the sweat.

# 诺贝尔文学奖获奖致辞

[美]威廉·福克纳 | 田辉 译

我认为这个奖项不是授予我个人的，而是授予我的工作的——一项毕生在人类精神的痛苦与汗水中进行的工作：既不为名，也不图利，而是要以人的精神为原料，创造出前所未有的东西。因此这个奖项我只是代为保管。要为这一奖项的奖金找到与其最初目的和意义相称的用处并不难。但我更欢迎这样做，利用这一时机，把这作为一个顶点，向那些已经献身于这一艰苦劳动的男女青年发出号召，他们中必定有人有一天会站到我现在站着的地方。

我们今天的悲剧是人们普遍存在的一种身体上的恐惧，这种恐惧存在已久，以至于我们已经习惯了。再也没有精神方面的问题。唯一的问题是：我什么时候会被炸得粉碎？正因如此，今天从事写作的青年男女已经忘记了处于矛盾冲突中的人类心灵问题，而这本身就能创造出好的作品，因为这是唯一值得去写、值得为之呕心沥血努力的题材。

He must learn them again. He must teach himself that the basest of all things is to be afraid; and, teaching himself that, forget it forever, leaving no room in his workshop for anything but the old verities and truths of the heart, the old universal truths lacking which any story is ephemeral and doomed—love and honour and pity and pride and compassion and sacrifice.

Until he does so, he labours under a curse. He writes not of love but of lust, of defeats in which nobody loses anything of value, of victories without hope and, worst of all, without pity or compassion. His griefs grieve on no universal bones, leaving no scars. He writes not of the heart but of the glands.

Until he relearns these things, he will write as though he stood among and watched the end of man. I decline to accept the end of man. It is easy enough to say that man is immortal simply because he will endure: that when the last ding-dong of doom has clanged and faded from the last worthless rock hanging tideless in the last red and dying evening, that even then there will still be one more sound: that of his puny inexhaustible voice, still talking.

人们必须重新认识这些问题，必须使自己明白，世间最可鄙的事情莫过于恐惧，一定告诫自己永远不要忘记，工作中除了关于心灵的古老真理之外，不要给任何东西留有空间。因为没有这些古老的普遍真理，任何故事都只是昙花一现，注定与成功无缘；这些真理就是爱、荣誉、怜悯、尊严、同情与牺牲。

　　若是做不到这样，将是白费气力。写出的爱情不是爱情，而是情欲；写出的失败是没有人失去可贵的东西的失败；写出的胜利希望渺茫，更糟的是，没有怜悯，也看不到同情；写出的悲伤脱离普世苍生，所以无关痛痒。写的不是心灵，而是分泌腺体的器官。

　　在人们重新了解这些之前，写作犹如站在处于世界末日的人类中看着末日的来临。我不接受世界末日的说法。不是简单地说人类能够持续就说人类是永恒的；当命运的最后钟声敲响，海上平静无浪，声音消失在映着落日余晖的最后一块无用的礁石旁时，还会有一种声音，那就是人类微弱不倦的争鸣。

I refuse to accept this. I believe that man will not merely endure: he will prevail. He is immortal, not because he alone among creatures has an inexhaustible voice, but because he has a soul, a spirit capable of compassion and sacrifice and endurance.

The poet's, the writer's, duty is to write about these things. It is his privilege to help man endure by lifting his heart, by reminding him of the courage and honour and hope and pride and compassion and pity and sacrifice which have been the glory of his past. The poet's voice need not merely be the record of man, it can be one of the props, the pillars to help him endure and prevail.

🐟 难词释义 ·······

commensurate [kə'menʃərət] *adj.* 相称的，相当的
pinnacle ['pɪnəkl] *n.* 顶点；顶峰
travail ['træveɪl] *n.* 艰苦劳动；艰辛
verity ['verəti] *n.* 准则，真理
ephemeral [ɪ'femərəl] *adj.* 短暂的；瞬息的
gland [glænd] *n.* 腺
puny ['pjuːni] *adj.* 弱小的
inexhaustible [ˌɪnɪɡ'zɔːstəbl] *adj.* 用之不竭的；无穷无尽的

我拒绝接受这种说法。我相信人类不仅能延续，而且能战胜一切。人类是永生的，不是因为在万物中唯有他的声音不会枯竭，而是因为他有灵魂，有同情心，有牺牲和忍耐精神。

诗人和作家的职责就是歌颂这些。通过鼓舞人的斗志，提醒他们牢记勇敢、荣誉、希望、尊严、同情、怜悯与牺牲精神——这些他们过去曾有过的殊荣——来帮助人类延续下去，这是诗人和作家的荣幸。诗人的声音不应该只是记录人类，而应是帮助人类持续和获胜的支柱。

威廉·福克纳（William Faulkner，1897—1962）

美国文学史上最具影响力的作家之一，意识流文学在美国的代表人物，诺贝尔文学奖获得者，一生共创作了多部长篇小说和短篇小说。代表作品有《喧哗与骚动》《我弥留之际》等。

# Learn to Live in the Present Moment

Richard Carlson

To a large degree, the measure about peace of mind is determined by how much we are able to live in the present moment. Irrespective of what happened yesterday or last year, and what may or may not happen tomorrow, the present moment is where you are—always.

Without question, many of us have mastered the neurotic art of spending much of our lives worrying about a variety of things—all at once. We allow past problems and future concerns to dominate our present moments, so much so that we end up being anxious, frustrated, depressed, and hopeless. On the flip side, we also postpone our gratification, our stated priorities, and our happiness, often convincing ourselves that "some day" will be better than today. Unfortunately, the same mental dynamics that tell us to look toward the future will only repeat themselves so that "some day" never actually arrives. John Lennon once said, "Life is what's happening while we're busy making other plans." When we're busy making "other plans", our children are busy growing up, the people we love are moving away and dying.

# 学会活在当下

[美] 理查德·卡尔森

我们的内心平和与否在很大程度上取决于我们是否可以活在当下。不管昨天或者去年发生了什么，也不管明天将要发生或者不发生什么，现当下才是你的生活所在——始终如此。

毫无疑问，我们中有很多人神经紧张，将生活中的大多数时间花在为各种事情担忧上——而且常常同时忧虑许多事情。我们任凭过去的问题和对未来的担心掌控我们现当下的生活，以至于我们整天焦虑不安，萎靡不振，甚至沮丧绝望。另一方面，我们又推迟自己获得满足感的时间，推迟应该优先考虑的事情，也推迟幸福感，还常常说服自己"有朝一日"会比今天更美好。遗憾的是，如此期许未来的精神动力只会周而复始地不断重复，于是"有朝一日"永远不会到来。约翰·列侬曾言："生活就是在我们忙于制订别的计划时发生的事。"当我们为制订种种"别的计划"而忙碌时，我们的孩子迅速成长，我们爱的人迁居他处，甚至撒手人寰。

Our bodies are getting out of shape, and our dreams are slipping away. In short, we miss out on life.

Many people live as if life were a dress rehearsal for some later date. It isn't. In fact, no one has a guarantee that he or she will be here tomorrow. Now is the only time we have, and the only time that we have any control over. When our attention is in the present moment, we push fear from our minds. Fear is the concern over events that might happen in the future—we won't have enough money, our children will get into trouble, we will get old and die, whatever.

To combat fear, the best strategy is to learn to bring your attention back to the present. Mark Twain said, "I have been through some terrible things in my life, some of which actually happened." I don't think I can say it any better. Practise keeping your attention on the here and now, your efforts will pay great dividends.

🐦 难词释义

irrespective [ˌɪrɪ'spektɪv] *adj.* 不考虑的；无关的
gratification [ˌɡrætɪfɪ'keɪʃn] *n.* 满足；满意
pay dividends 有回报

我们的身材逐渐走样，梦想悄然溜走。总之，我们错过了生活。

许多人的生活仿佛是未来某个日子的彩排，事实却并非如此。实际上，没有人能保证他或她明天还健在。现当下是我们唯一能拥有的时间，也是我们唯一可以掌控的时间。当我们将注意力放在当下，就不会再感到恐惧。所谓恐惧，就是我们对未来会发生某些事情的担忧——我们的钱不够花，我们的孩子会陷入困境，我们会变老，会死去，诸如此类。

要克服恐惧心理，最佳策略就是学会把你的注意力拉回到当下。马克·吐温曾说过："我的一生经历过一些可怕的事情，部分的确发生过。"我认为我说不出比这更具内涵的话语。不妨练习将注意力集中于此情此景、此时此刻，你的努力终会有丰厚的回报。

理查德·卡尔森（Richard Carlson，1961—2006）

--------

美国首屈一指的心理咨询专家、演讲家，毕生致力于幸福和减压方面的研究。著有《别再为小事抓狂》系列等30余本图书，著作被翻译成35种语言，在130多个国家出版，指导了数千万人将书中的"不抓狂"理念落实到现实生活中，进而创造和谐而美好的人生。

# The Goodness of Life

Ralph Marston

Though there is much to be concerned about, there is far, far more for which to be thankful. Though life's goodness can at times be overshadowed, it is never outweighed.

For every single act that is senselessly destructive, there are thousands more small, quiet acts of love, kindness and compassion. For every person who seeks to hurt, there are many, many more who devote their lives to helping and to healing.

There is goodness to life that cannot be denied.

In the most magnificent vistas and in the smallest details, look closely, for that goodness always comes shining through.

There is no limit to the goodness of life. It grows more abundant with each new encounter. The more you experience and appreciate the goodness of life, the more there is to be lived.

Even when the cold winds blow and the world seems to be covered in foggy shadows, the goodness of life lives on. Open your eyes, open your heart, and you will see that goodness is everywhere.

# 生命的美好

［美］拉尔夫·马斯顿

尽管有很多事让人忧虑，但相比而言，值得感激的事要多得多。尽管生命的美好有时会被蒙上阴影，但它永远不会被埋没。

相对于每一个无谓的破坏行为而言，有更多数以千计微小的，包含着爱、友善和同情的举动在静静地上演。相对于每一个试图伤害他人的人而言，都有更多的人在用他们的生命去帮助和治愈他人。

生命的美好不可否认。

在最为宏伟的愿景和最为琐碎的细节中，请仔细观察，因为美好的事物总是散发着耀眼的光芒闪亮登场。

生命的美好是无限的。它会随着每一次新的相遇而变得越发丰富。你经历得越多，越能欣赏生命的美好，那么，你生命中的美好就会越多。

即使寒风凛冽，整个世界似乎都被雾霭笼罩，生命的美好依然存在。睁开双眼，打开心扉，你会发现美好无处不在。

Though the goodness of life seems at times to suffer setbacks, it always endures. For in the darkest moment it becomes vividly clear that life is a priceless treasure. And so the goodness of life is made even stronger by the very things that would oppose it.

Time and time again when you feared it was gone forever, you found that the goodness of life was really only a moment away. Around the next corner, inside every moment, the goodness of life is there to surprise and delight you.

Take a moment to let the goodness of life touch your spirit and calm your thoughts. Then, share your good fortune with another. For the goodness of life grows more and more magnificent each time it is given away.

Though the problems constantly scream for attention and the conflicts appear to rage ever stronger, the goodness of life grows stronger still, quietly, peacefully, with more purpose and meaning than ever before.

📖 难词释义

overshadow [ˌəʊvəˈʃædəʊ] *v.* 使蒙上阴影
abundant [əˈbʌndənt] *adj.* 大量的；丰盛的

尽管生命的美好有时似乎遭受挫折，但它总能挺过来。因为在最黑暗的时刻，有一点变得格外明晰，那就是，生命是无价之宝。可见，正是与生命的美好相对立的事物使其变得越发强大。

一次又一次，当你担心这美好永远离你而去时，你会发现，生命的美好其实只与你相隔须臾。它就在下一个角落，在每一刻，等着给你惊喜和快乐。

花些时间让生命的美好触动你的灵魂，抚平你的思绪。然后，与他人分享你的好运。因为每次给予都会让生命的美好变得更加壮丽。

尽管总是有问题强烈地想要引人注意，冲突也似乎愈演愈烈，但生命的美好却静静地、平和地，带着比以往任何时候都更强的意志和更高的价值变得更加强大。

拉尔夫·马斯顿（Ralph Marston，1907—1967）

......

美国作家、励志演说家，写作风格以简单易懂而闻名，最广为人知的作品为《每日激励》，书中涵盖了各种主题，在无数寻求生活动力和建议的听众中引起了巨大反响，他本人也因此成了自助和个人发展领域的首选人物。

形色人生
Human Life

# Six Famous Words

## William Lyon Phelps

"To be or not to be." Outside the *Bible*, these six words are the most famous in all the literature of the world. They were spoken by Hamlet when he was thinking aloud, and they are the most famous words in Shakespeare because Hamlet was speaking not only for himself but for every thinking man and woman. To be or not to be—to live or not to live, to live richly and abundantly and eagerly, or to live dully and meanly and scarcely. A philosopher once wanted to know whether he was alive or not, which is a good question for everyone to put to himself occasionally. He answered it by saying: "I think, therefore I am."

But the best definition of existence I ever saw was one written by another philosopher who said: "To be is to be in relations." If this is true, then the more relations a living thing has, the more it is alive. To live abundantly means simply to increase the range and intensity of our relations. Unfortunately, we are so constituted that we get to love our routine. But apart from our regular occupation how much are we alive? If you are interested only in your regular occupation, you are alive only to that extent.

# 六字名言

[美] 威廉·莱昂·费尔普斯

"生存还是毁灭",如果把《圣经》除外,这六个字当数世界文学中最有名的六个字。这句话是哈姆雷特在一次喃喃自语时说的,也是莎士比亚作品中最有名的词句,因为哈姆雷特不仅道出了自己的心声,也道出了每一个有思想的男男女女的心声。生存还是毁灭——是要生活还是不要生活,是活得丰富、充实、兴致勃勃,还是活得枯燥、吝啬、贫乏无味。一位哲学家曾想弄清自己是否活着,这个问题我们每个人也应当时不时地问问自己。他想出的答案是:"我思故我在。"

但是我看到的关于生存的最佳定义是另一位哲学家所写的:"生存即是联系。"如果这话不假,那么一个有生命的东西建立的联系越多,它就越有生气。所谓活得丰富充实也仅是扩大和加强我们的各种联系。不幸的是,天性使得我们喜欢墨守成规。试问除去日常工作,我们又有多少时间是活着的呢?如果你只对自己的日常工作有兴趣,那你的生命也就局限于此了。

So far as other things are concerned—poetry and prose, music, pictures, sports, unselfish friendships, politics, international affairs—you are dead.

Contrariwise, it is true that every time you acquire a new interest—even more, a new accomplishment—you increase your power of life. No one who is deeply interested in a large variety of subjects can remain unhappy; the real pessimist is the person who has lost interest.

Bacon said that a man dies as often as he loses a friend. But we gain new life by contacts, new friends. What is supremely true of living objects is only less true of ideas, which are also alive. Where your thoughts are, there will your life be also. If your thoughts are confined only to your business, only to your physical welfare, only to the narrow circle of the town in which you live, then you live in a narrow circumscribed life. But if you are interested in what is going on in China, then you are living in China; if you are interested in the characters of a good novel, then you are living with those highly interesting people; if you listen intently to fine music, you are away from your immediate surroundings and living in a world of passion and imagination.

至于其他方面——比如诗歌、散文、音乐、绘画、体育、无私的友谊、政治与国际事务等等——你只是死人一个。

但反过来说，每当你习得一种新的兴趣——甚至是获得一项新的成就——你的生命力就增强了。一个对诸多事物都很有兴趣的人是不可能不快乐的，真正的悲观主义者是那些失去兴趣的人。

培根说过，一个人失去一个朋友，就是经历一次死亡。但是通过交往和结识新朋友，我们就能获得新生。这条对人而言千真万确的道理在一定程度上也适用于人的思想，因为它也是有生命的。你的思想所在，便是你的生命所在。如果你的思想只局限于你的事业，只局限于你的物质利益，跳不出生活居所所在地的小圈子，那么你的一生便处处受限，在狭隘中度过。但是如果你对中国正在发生的种种事情感兴趣，那你就是在中国生活；如果你对一本出色的小说中的人物感兴趣，那你便是活在一群非常有趣的人中间；如果你能全神贯注地聆听高雅的音乐，那你就能远离周遭的环境，生活在一个充满激情与想象的世界里。

To be or not to be—to live intensely and richly, or merely to exist, that depends on ourselves. Let us widen and intensify our relations. While we live, let us live!

 难词释义

contrariwise [kən'treəriwaɪz] *adv.* 反之，相反
circumscribe ['sɜːkəmskraɪb] *v.* 限制，约束
intensify [ɪn'tensɪfaɪ] *v.* 加剧，增强

生存还是毁灭——是活得热烈而丰富，还是仅仅存在就行，取决于我们自己。但愿我们都能不断扩宽和增强联系。既然我们活着，就活得热烈吧！

**威廉·莱昂·费尔普斯**（William Lyon Phelps，1865—1943）

美国作家、评论家和学者。他在美国大学开设了第一门现代小说课程，并为报纸写专栏，还在杂志和期刊上发表了许多文章，为普及当代文学教学做出了很大贡献。

# Human Life a Poem (I)

Lin Yutang

I think that, from a biological standpoint, human life almost reads like a poem. It has its own rhythm and beat, its internal cycles of growth and decay. It begins with innocent childhood, followed by awkward adolescence trying awkwardly to adapt itself to mature society, with its young passions and follies, its ideals and ambitions; then it reaches a manhood of intense activities, profiting from experience and learning more about society and human nature; at middle age, there is a slight easing of tension, a mellowing of character like the ripening of fruit or the mellowing of good wine, and the gradual acquiring of a more tolerant, more cynical and at the same time a kindlier view of life; then in the sunset of our life, the endocrine glands decrease their activity, and if we have a true philosophy of old age and have ordered our life pattern according to it, it is for us the age of peace and security and leisure and contentment; finally, life flickers out and one goes into eternal sleep, never to wake up again.

# 人生如诗（一）

林语堂 ｜ 乌日娜 译

　　我觉得，从生物学的角度来看，人的一生恰如一首诗。人生自有其韵律和节奏，自有其内在的生长与衰亡规律。人生始于无邪的童年，经过少年的青涩，带着激情与无知、理想与雄心，笨拙而努力地走向成熟；后来人到壮年，经历渐广，阅人渐多，涉世渐深，收益也渐大；及至中年，人生的紧张得以舒缓，人的性格日渐成熟，如芳馥之果实，如醇美之佳酿，更具容忍之心，处世虽更悲观，但对人生的态度趋于和善；再后来就是人生迟暮，内分泌系统活动减少，若此时吾辈已经悟得老年真谛，并据此安排生活，那生活将和平、宁静、安详而知足；最后，生命之烛摇曳而终熄灭，人进入永恒的长眠，不再醒来。

One should be able to sense the beauty of this rhythm of life, to appreciate, as we do in grand symphonies, its main theme, its strains of conflict and the final resolution. The movements of these cycles are very much the same in a normal life, but the music must be provided by the individual himself.

🐦 难词释义

mellow ['meləʊ] v. （使）成熟
endocrine ['endəkrɪn] adj. 内分泌的

人应当学会感受生命的韵律之美，像听交响乐一样，欣赏其主旋律、激昂的高潮和舒缓的尾声。这些反复的乐章于我们的生命而言都大同小异，但每个人的乐曲却需要自己去谱写。

## 林语堂（Lin Yutang，1895—1976）

中国现代著名作家、学者、翻译家、语言学家。早年留学美国、德国，获哈佛大学文学硕士、莱比锡大学语言学博士。林语堂于1940年和1950年先后两度获得诺贝尔文学奖提名。其作品包括小说《京华烟云》《啼笑皆非》，散文和杂文文集《人生的盛宴》《生活的艺术》等。

# Three Days to See (Excerpts)

Helen Keller

All of us have read thrilling stories in which the hero had only a limited and specified time to live. Sometimes it was as long as a year, sometimes as short as 24 hours. But always we were interested in discovering just how the doomed hero chose to spend his last days or his last hours. I speak, of course, of free men who have a choice, not condemned criminals whose sphere of activities is strictly delimited.

Such stories set us thinking, wondering what we should do under similar circumstances. What events, what experiences, what associations should we crowd into those last hours as mortal beings? What happiness should we find in reviewing the past, what regrets?

Sometimes I have thought it would be an excellent rule to live each day as if we should die tomorrow. Such an attitude would emphasise sharply the values of life. We should live each day with gentleness, vigor and a keenness of appreciation which are often lost when time stretches before us in the constant panorama of more days and months and years to come.

# 假如给我三天光明（节选）

[美] 海伦·凯勒

我们都读过那种扣人心弦的故事，故事中的主人公将不久于人世，有剩一年时间的，也有只剩 24 小时的。但我们总是想知道，注定要离世的人会选择如何度过自己最后的时光。当然，我说的是那些有选择权利的自由人，而不是那些活动范围受到严格限制的死刑犯。

这样的故事让我们思考，在类似的处境下，我们应该做些什么。人终有一死，在最后的几个小时里，我们应该做些什么，体验些什么，或者与什么人联系？回忆往昔，什么能使我们开心快乐？什么又使我们悔恨不已？

有时我想，把每一天都当作生命的最后一天来过，也不失为一种极好的生活法则。这种态度会使人格外重视生命的价值。我们每天都应该怀着感恩之心，姿态优雅、朝气蓬勃地生活。但当时间在我们面前日复一日、月复一月、年复一年地流逝时，我们常常会弄丢这种态度。

There are those, of course, who would adopt the epicurean motto of "Eat, drink, and be merry." But most people would be chastened by the certainty of impending death.

In stories the doomed hero is usually saved at the last minute by some stroke of fortune, but almost always his sense of values is changed. He becomes more appreciative of the meaning of life and its permanent spiritual values. It has often been noted that those who live, or have lived, in the shadow of death bring a mellow sweetness to everything they do.

Most of us, however, take life for granted. We know that one day we must die, but usually we picture that day as far in the future. When we are in buoyant health, death is all but unimaginable. We seldom think of it. The days stretch out in an endless vista. So we go about our petty tasks, hardly aware of our listless attitude toward life.

The same lethargy, I am afraid, characterises the use of all our faculties and senses. Only the deaf appreciate hearing, only the blind realise the manifold blessings that lie in sight.

当然，也有人奉行"吃喝玩乐"的享乐主义信条，但绝大多数人还是会在死亡即将到来之时感到懊悔。

在故事中，将死的主人公通常在最后一刻因机缘巧合而获救，但他的价值观通常也会发生改变。他变得更加懂得生命的意义及其永恒的精神价值。我们常常注意到，那些生活在或曾经生活在死亡阴影下的人，无论做什么都会感到幸福。

然而，我们中的大多数人都把生命看成是理所当然的。我们知道有一天我们终将面对死亡，但总认为那一天还在遥远的将来。当我们身强体健之时，死亡简直不可想象，我们很少想到它。日子多得好像没有尽头。于是我们一味忙于琐事，几乎意识不到我们对待生活的态度有多冷漠。

恐怕我们对自身官能和感觉的运用也是如此冷漠吧。只有失聪者才了解听力的重要，只有失明者才明白视力的可贵。

Particularly does this observation apply to those who have lost sight and hearing in adult life. But those who have never suffered impairment of sight or hearing seldom make the fullest use of these blessed faculties. Their eyes and ears take in all sights and sounds hazily, without concentration and with little appreciation. It is the same old story of not being grateful for what we have until we lose it, of not being conscious of health until we are ill.

I have often thought it would be a blessing if each human being were stricken blind and deaf for a few days at some time during his early adult life. Darkness would make him more appreciative of sight; silence would teach him the joys of sound.

🐦 难词释义 ·······································································•

panorama [ˌpænə'rɑːmə] *n.* 全景
epicurean [ˌepɪkjʊə'riːən] *adj.* 享乐的；吃喝玩乐的
chasten ['tʃeɪsn] *v.* 使内疚；使懊悔
impending [ɪm'pendɪŋ] *adj.* 即将发生的；迫在眉睫的
buoyant ['bɔɪənt] *adj.* 繁荣的；乐观的
lethargy ['leθədʒi] *n.* 冷漠；无精打采
manifold ['mænɪfəʊld] *adj.* 多的；多种多样的
impairment [ɪm'peəmənt] *n.* 缺陷，障碍，损伤

那些成年后才失去视力或听力的人对此感受尤为深刻。但那些从来没有遭受过视力或听力障碍的人很少会充分利用这些宝贵的能力。他们的眼睛和耳朵模糊地接收着周围的景物与声音，心不在焉，也无所感激。这和我们只有在失去后才懂得珍惜一样，我们只有在生病时才意识到健康的可贵。

我常常想，如果每个人在年轻的时候都有几天失明或失聪的经历，也不失为一件幸事。黑暗会使他更加珍惜光明，哑默会教导他更喜慕声音。

海伦·凯勒（Helen Keller，1880—1968）

美国知名女作家、教育家、慈善家、社会活动家。她在出生 19 个月后因疾病被夺去视力和听力。在无光、无声的世界里，她先后完成了 14 本著作。代表作有《假如给我三天光明》《我的生活故事》《石墙之歌》等。

# On Meeting the Celebrated

William Somerset Maugham

I have always wondered at the passion many people have to meet the celebrated. The prestige you acquire by being able to tell your friends that you know famous men proves only that you are yourself of small account. The celebrated develop a technique to deal with the persons they come across. They show the world a mask, often an impressive one, but take care to conceal their real selves. They play the part that is expected from them, and with practice learn to play it very well, but you are stupid if you think that this public performance of theirs corresponds with the man within.

I have been attached, deeply attached, to a few people; but I have been interested in men in general not for their own sakes, but for the sake of my work. I have not, as Kant enjoined, regarded each man as an end in himself, but as material that might be useful to me as a writer. I have been more concerned with the obscure than with the famous. They are more often themselves. They have had no need to create a figure to protect themselves from the world or to impress it. Their idiosyncrasies have had more chance to develop in the limited circle of their activity,

# 论见名人

[英]威廉·萨默塞特·毛姆 | 周成刚 译

许多人热衷于见名人，我始终不得其解。在朋友面前吹嘘自己认识某某名人，由此而来的声望只能证明自己的微不足道。名人个个练就了一套处世高招，无论遇上谁，都能应付自如。他们给世人展现的是一副样子，而且常常是美好难忘的那种，但他们也会小心翼翼地掩盖自己真实的模样。他们扮演的是大家期待他们演的角色，演得多了，最后都能演得惟妙惟肖。如果你以为他们展现在公众面前的形象就是他们真实的自我，那你就太傻了。

我自己就喜欢一些人，而且是非常喜欢的那种。但我对人感兴趣一般不是因为他们自身的缘故，而是出于我个人工作的需求。正如康德劝告的那样，我从来没有把认识某人作为目的，而是将其视为对作家有用的创作素材。比起名流显士，我更关注无名小卒。他们常常显得更加真实自然，无须另外再创造一个人物形象来保护自己不受世人干扰，抑或惊艳世人。他们的社交圈子有限，种种癖性有更多空间得到滋长。

and since they have never been in the public eye it has never occurred to them that they have anything to conceal. They display their oddities because it has never struck them that they are odd. And after all it is with the common run of men that we writers have to deal; kings, dictators, commercial magnates are from our point of view very unsatisfactory. To write about them is a venture that has often tempted writers, but the failure that has attended their efforts shows that such beings are too exceptional to form a proper ground for a work of art. They cannot be made real. The ordinary is the writer's richer field. Its unexpectedness, its singularity, its infinite variety afford unending material. The great man is too often all of a piece; it is the little man that is a bundle of contradictory elements. He is inexhaustible. You never come to the end of the surprises he has in store for you. For my part I would much sooner spend a month on a desert island with a veterinary surgeon than with a prime minister.

---

### 🐟 难词释义

enjoin [ɪn'dʒɔɪn] *v.* 嘱咐；责令
idiosyncrasy [ˌɪdiə'sɪŋkrəsi] *n.* （个人特有的）癖好；特征；习性
oddity ['ɒdəti] *n.* 古怪反常的人（或事物）；古怪
magnate ['mæɡneɪt] *n.* 权贵；要人；（尤指）产业大亨

因为他们从来没有引起公众的关注，也就从来没有想过要隐瞒什么。他们会表露自己古怪的一面，因为他们从来就没有觉得自己有何古怪。毕竟，作家要写的是普通人。在我们看来，国王、独裁者和商界大亨这些都是不符合条件的。去撰写这些人物经常是作家们难以抗拒的冒险之举，但为此付出的努力不免以失败告终，可见这些人物都过于特殊，无法成为艺术作品的创作根基，作家也不可能把他们写得真真切切。普通人才是作家的创作沃土，他们或变幻无常，或难觅其二，各式人物应有尽有，给作家提供了无限的创作素材。大人物经常是千人一面，小人物身上才自带层层矛盾元素，是取之不尽的创作源泉，让你惊喜不断。就我而言，如果要在荒岛上度过一个月，我宁愿和一名兽医相守，也不愿同一位首相做伴。

**威廉·萨默塞特·毛姆**（William Somerset Maugham，1874—1965）

英国小说家、剧作家。代表作有长篇小说《人性的枷锁》《月亮和六便士》，短篇小说集《叶之震颤》《阿金》等。

# Companionship of Books

Samuel Smiles

A man may usually be known by the books he reads as well as by the company he keeps; for there is a companionship of books as well as of men; and one should always live in the best company, whether it be of books or of men.

A good book may be among the best of friends. It is the same today that it always was, and it will never change. It is the most patient and cheerful of companions. It does not turn its back upon us in times of adversity or distress. It always receives us with the same kindness, amusing and instructing us in youth, and comforting and consoling us in age.

Men often discover their affinity to each other by the mutual love they have for a book just as two persons sometimes discover a friend by the admiration which both entertain for a third. There is an old proverb, "Love me, love my dog." But there is more wisdom in this: "Love me, love my book." The book is a truer and higher bond of union. Men can think, feel, and sympathise with each other through their favourite author. They live in him together, and he in them.

# 以书为伴

[英] 塞缪尔·斯迈尔斯

通常，要了解一个人的为人，可以去看他读些什么书，与什么人交往。因为有人以书为伴，有人以人为伴。无论是书还是人，我们都应坚持择其佳者。

一本好书就如同一位益友。它始终如一，不曾改变，是最耐心、最令人愉悦的伴侣。在我们身处困境、苦恼忧伤之时，它不会抛弃我们，而是一如既往，仁慈以对。在我们年轻时，它给予我们快乐，传授我们知识；在我们年老时，它又给予我们慰藉和勉励。

人们常因喜欢同一本书而结为知己，就像两个人因为钦佩同一个人而成为朋友。古语云，"爱屋及乌"。但我认为"爱吾及书"更富哲理。书是更为真诚而高尚的情谊纽带。人们可以通过共同喜爱的作家沟通思想，交流感情，产生共鸣。彼此情感相通，思想相融。

A good book is often the best urn of a life enshrining the best that life could think out; for the world of a man's life is, for the most part, but the world of his thoughts. Thus the best books are treasuries of good words, the golden thoughts, which, remembered and cherished, become our constant companions and comforters.

Books possess an essence of immortality. They are by far the most lasting products of human effort. Temples and statues decay, but books survive. Time is of no account with great thoughts, which are as fresh today as when they first passed through their author's minds, ages ago. What was then said and thought still speaks to us as vividly as ever from the printed page. The only effect of time have been to sift out the bad products; for nothing in literature can long survive but what is really good.

Books introduce us into the best society; they bring us into the presence of the greatest minds that have ever lived. We hear what they said and did; we see them as if they were really alive; we sympathise with them, enjoy with them, grieve with them; their experience becomes ours, and we feel as if we were in a measure actors with them in the scenes which they describe.

好书如同最珍贵的宝器，珍藏着一个人一生思想之精华，因为一个人的人生境界主要就是其思想的境界。因此，好书恰似良言与宝贵思想的宝库。这些良言和思想若被我们铭记于心并多加珍视，就会成为我们永远的陪伴和慰藉。

书籍具有不朽的性质，是人类迄今为止努力创造出的最为持久的产物。寺庙会坍塌，神像会朽烂，但书籍可以永存。时间的影响在伟大的思想面前无关紧要。多年前闪现于作者脑海里的伟大思想现如今依然清新如故。书中所记载的文字和思想依然生动如初，向我们娓娓道来。时间于书籍的唯一作用就是淘汰不好的作品，因为只有真正的佳作才能长存。

书籍让我们得以与最优秀的人为伴，将我们置身于历代伟人巨匠之间，如闻其声，如观其行，如见其人；和他们产生共鸣，共享悲喜，感同身受。在一定程度上，我们好像皆成了他们所绘场景中的演员，正与他们一起登台亮相。

The great and good do not die, even in this world. Embalmed in books, their spirits walk abroad. The book is a living voice. It is an intellect to which one still listens. Hence we ever remain under the influence of the great men of old. The imperial intellects of the world are as much alive now as they were ages ago.

## 难词释义

affinity [əˈfɪnəti] *n.* 喜爱；类同
urn [ɜːn] *n.* 瓮
enshrine [ɪnˈʃraɪn] *v.* 珍藏
sift out 淘汰；筛除
embalm [ɪmˈbɑːm] *v.* 使不朽；铭记于心

纵使是在这人世间，伟人们也可以长存。他们的精神被载入书册，传遍四海。书是人们至今仍然能聆听到的智慧之声，永远充满着活力。于是我们一直都受历代伟人的影响。多少世纪以前的盖世英才，如今仍同当年一样，焕发着强大的生命力。

塞缪尔·斯迈尔斯（Samuel Smiles，1812—1904）

英国 19 世纪伟大的道德学家、著名的社会改革家和散文随笔作家。他的作品主要有《自己拯救自己》《品格的力量》《金钱与人生》《命运之门》《信仰的力量》等。

# Love Is Difficult

## Rainer Maria Rilke

It is good to love, but love is difficult. For one human being to
love another human being: that is perhaps the most difficult task
that has been entrusted to us, the ultimate task, the final test and
proof, the work for which all other work is merely preparation.
That is why young people, who are beginners in everything, are
not yet capable of love: it is something they must learn. With
their whole being, with all their forces, gathered around their
solitary, anxious, upward-beating heart, they must learn to love.
But learning time is always a long, secluded time ahead and far on
into life, is solitude, a heightened and deepened kind of aloneness
for the person who loves. Loving does not at first mean merging,
surrendering or uniting with another person (what would a union
be for two people who are unclarified, unfinished, and still
incoherent?); it is a high inducement for the individual to ripen,
to become something in himself, to become world, to become
world in himself for the sake of another person; it is a great,

# 爱，是艰难的

[奥] 赖纳·马里亚·里尔克

爱很美好，但爱是艰难的。因为让一个人去爱另一个人，这也许是我们被赋予的最艰难的任务，是终极任务，也是最后的考验和证明，其他所有的努力都只是为此做的准备。这就是那些一切都才刚刚开始的年轻人没有爱的能力的原因：爱是他们必须要学习的东西。他们必须耐住孤独，克服焦虑，怀着一颗进取的心用尽全力去学习爱。在这个漫长而又隐蔽的学习过程中，生命深处的底色是孤独。对具有爱的能力的人而言，那种孤独更加崇高，也更加深沉。爱并不是一开始就意味着与人合二为一、向人臣服或通力合作（对两个懵懂无知、未经世事、话都说不清楚的人来说，那会是怎样的一种结合呢？）。爱对一个人而言具有强烈的吸引力，吸引着人们变得成熟，努力完善自己，活出一方天地，丰富阅历，娱人悦己；爱是一种伟大

demanding claim on him, something that chooses him and calls him to vast distances. Only in this sense, as the task of working on themselves (to hearken and to hammer day and night), may young people use the love that is given to them. Merging and surrendering and every kind of communion is not for them (who must still, for a long, long time, save and gather themselves), it is the ultimate, is perhaps that for which human lives as yet barely large enough.

🐟 难词释义 ............................................... •

secluded [sɪ'kluːdɪd] *adj.* 隐蔽的；隐退的
inducement [ɪn'djuːsmənt] *n.* 诱因，刺激
communion [kə'mjuːniən] *n.* （思想感情的）交融，交流

而苛刻的宣言，对一个人提出要求并且呼唤着他走向远方。只有在这种意义上，年轻人才会把爱当作提升自己的未尽工作（昼夜不停地探索、锤炼）。至于与人合二为一、向人臣服以及各种各样的交融合作，还不是他们能做到的（在很长、很长一段时间里，他们还必须提升自己，打起精神），那是最后的终点，又或许是人类至今还未能达到的境界。

赖纳·马里亚·里尔克（Rainer Maria Rilke，1875—1926）

　　奥地利诗人，其创作内涵及表现形式深邃而复杂，扩大了诗歌的艺术表现领域，对欧洲现代诗歌的发展产生了巨大影响，本人也因《杜伊诺挽歌》和《致俄耳甫斯的十四行诗》等作品而享誉国际。

# On Marriage

Gibran Kahlil Gibran

Then Almitra spoke again and said, "And what of Marriage, master?"

And he answered saying:

"You were born together, and together you shall be forevermore.

You shall be together when the white wings of death scatter your days.

Ay, you shall be together even in the silent memory of God.

But let there be spaces in your togetherness,

And let the winds of the heavens dance between you.

Love one another, but make not a bond of love:

Let it rather be a moving sea between the shores of your souls.

Fill each other's cup but drink not from one cup.

Give one another of your bread but eat not from the same loaf.

Sing and dance together and be joyous, but let each one of you be alone,

# 论婚姻

［黎］纪伯伦·哈利勒·纪伯伦

听闻此言，艾尔·米特拉接着问道：先知啊，什么是婚姻的真谛？

他答道：

"你们结伴而生，亦将相伴永远。

你们彼此相伴，哪怕死神的白色羽翼令你们的日子零落分散。

是啊，即便在神静默的记忆中，你们也应彼此相伴。
但要切记，契合之中须有空间。
好让天堂之风，在彼此之间翩跹。

彼此须当相爱，却不可将爱变成绑缚：
要让爱成为浩瀚汪洋，在彼此灵魂的海岸之间起伏。

斟满彼此的杯盏，却不可同饮一盏。
以面包互赠，却不可共食一片。

一起欢歌曼舞，各自也要独立孑然，

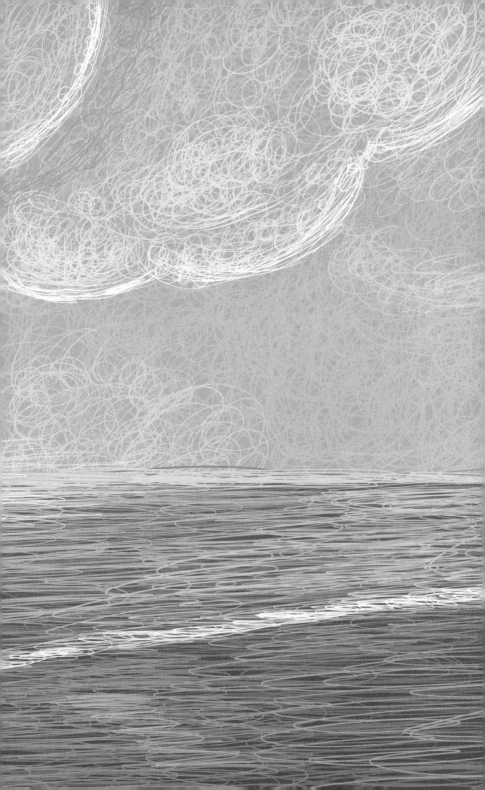

"Even as the strings of the lute are alone though they quiver with the same music.

Give your hearts, but not into each other's keeping.

For only the hand of Life can contain your hearts.

And stand together yet not too near together:

For the pillars of the temple stand apart,

And the oak tree and the cypress grow not in each other's shadow."

难词释义

lute [luːt] *n.* 琉特琴，诗琴（拨弦乐器）
cypress ['saɪprəs] *n.* 柏树

"正如琉特琴琴弦，一根根各自分明，哪怕它们为同一段旋律震颤。

交出你们的心，却不可托付对方收存。

只有生命之手，才能容下你们的心。

要并肩而立，却不可靠得太近：

要知道，殿宇的廊柱皆有间距，

橡树和柏树也不会托庇于彼此的树荫。"

纪伯伦·哈利勒·纪伯伦（Gibran Kahlil Gibran，1883—1931）

黎巴嫩作家、诗人、画家，阿拉伯文学的主要奠基人。主要作品有《泪与笑》《先知》《沙与沫》等。这篇《论婚姻》选自他的巅峰之作《先知》。

# A Straight Wall Is Hard to Build (Excerpts)

Lou R. Crandall

As I try to outline my thoughts, the subject becomes more and more difficult. I have many basic beliefs but as I try to pick and choose it seems to me that they all can be summarised in the word "character". Obviously, what you believe is a fundamental thing. There can be no fanfare, no embellishments. It must be honest.

An architect once told me that the most difficult structure to design was a simple monumental shaft. The proportions must be perfect to be pleasing. The hardest thing to build is a plain straight wall. The dimensions must be absolute. In either case there is no ornamentation to hide irregularities, no moldings to cover hidden defects and no supports to strengthen concealed weaknesses.

I am using this example to illustrate human character, which to me is the most important single power in the world today. The young people of toady are in reality foundations of structures yet to be built. It is obvious that the design of these human structures is the combined efforts of many human architects. Boys and girls

# 人格的力量（节选）

［美］卢·R.克兰德尔

在我努力厘清思路时，主题变得越来越难讲述。我有诸多基本信仰，但是当我试图从中挑选时，发现它们似乎都可以用"人格"这个词来概括。很明显，一个人的信仰是最根本的东西，无须炫耀，无须修饰，是什么就是什么。

一位建筑师曾告诉我，最难设计的建筑是一尊简单的纪念柱，比例必须完美无缺才能赏心悦目；最难建造的是一堵平直的墙，尺寸必须分毫不差。不管是哪一种场景，都无法用修饰来掩盖不平整，无法用造型来遮盖暗藏的缺陷，也不能以支撑物来加固不牢的根基。

我以此例来说明人格，因为在我看来，人格是当今世界最重要的一种力量。今天的年轻人实际上就是世界待建结构的根基。显然，如何设计这些结构离不开众多人类建筑师的共同努力。孩子们的成长，

are influenced first by their parents, then by their friends and finally by business associates. During this period of construction, the human character is revised and changed until at maturity a fairly well-fixed form of character is found.

There are few human straight walls and fewer human monumental shafts. Such men and women are personalities of great beauty and are so rare that history records their being and holds them up as examples for the future. The Biblical characters are for me the closest examples of human perfection. They were unselfish, steadfast in their faith and unstinting in their help to others.

Today in this world of turmoil and trouble we could use more of such people, but they do not just happen along. I believe that they are the result of concentrated effort on the part of parents and associates, and the more we build with character the better the world will become. This may sound like a dreamer's hope and a theoretical goal which can never be reached. I do not think so.

 难词释义

fanfare ['fænfeə(r)] *n.* 大张旗鼓的宣传
embellishment [ɪm'belɪʃmənt] *n.* 美化；装饰
unstinting [ʌn'stɪntɪŋ] *adj.* 慷慨的；大方的

先后要受到父母、朋友和事业伙伴的影响。在这一成长过程中，人格一直在改变，直到在成熟期基本定型。

像墙一般笔直挺立的人少有，像纪念柱一样矗立的人更少，这样的人是美的化身，举世罕见，所以历史记载了他们的存在，奉其为后世之楷模。《圣经》中的人物在我心中是最接近完人的范例，他们无私，信仰坚定，而且帮助他人时不遗余力。

在如今这个动荡不安的世界，我们需要更多这样的人，但他们并非从天而降。我相信他们是父母和同伴共同努力塑造的结果。我们越重视人格的建构，世界就会越美好。这听起来像是痴人说梦，又好似一个永远无法实现的理论目标，但我却不这么认为。

# Professions for Women

Virginia Woolf

When your secretary invited me to come here, she told me that your Society is concerned with the employment of women and she suggested that I might tell you something about my own professional experiences. It is true I am a woman; it is true I am employed; but what professional experiences have I had? It is difficult to say. My profession is literature; and in that profession there are fewer experiences for women than in any other, with the exception of the stage—fewer, I mean, that are peculiar to women. For the road was cut many years ago—by Fanny Burney, by Aphra Behn, by Harriet Martineau, by Jane Austen, by George Eliot—many famous women, and many more unknown and forgotten, have been before me, making the path smooth, and regulating my steps. Thus, when I came to write, there were very few material obstacles in my way. Writing was a reputable and harmless occupation. The family peace was not broken by the scratching of a pen. No demand was made upon the family purse. For ten and sixpence one can buy paper enough to write all the plays of Shakespeare—if one has a mind that way.

# 女性的职业

[英] 弗吉尼亚·伍尔夫

贵团体秘书邀请我来这里时告诉我，你们在关注女性就业问题。她建议我或许可以和你们聊聊我自己的职业经历。不错，我的确是一名女性，我也的确有工作，但我能有什么职业经历呢？这很难说。我从事的是文学创作，在这份职业中，除了戏剧创作之外，女性能经历的事情比其他职业都少——我的意思是，很少有什么经历为女性所特有。因为这条路是很多年前开辟的，范妮·伯尼、阿芙拉·贝恩、哈丽雅特·马蒂诺、简·奥斯汀和乔治·艾略特——这些知名女性以及更多不为人所知、被遗忘的女性在我之前已将该路铺平，指引着我的脚步。因此，当我开始写作时，几乎没有遇到什么实际的障碍。写作是一份体面而无害的职业。家庭和谐不会因动笔书写时的沙沙声而破裂。也不需要什么家庭开销。花十先令六便士就能买到一大堆纸，足以写完莎士比亚的所有戏剧——如果谁想这样做的话。

Pianos and models, Paris, Vienna and Berlin, masters and mistresses, are not needed by a writer. The cheapness of writing paper is, of course, the reason why women have succeeded as writers before they have succeeded in the other professions.

But to tell you my story—it is a simple one. You have only got to figure to yourselves a girl in a bedroom with a pen in her hand. She had only to move that pen from left to right—from ten o'clock to one. Then it occurred to her to do what is simple and cheap enough after all—to slip a few of those pages into an envelope, fix a penny stamp in the corner, and drop the envelope into the red box at the corner. It was thus that I became a journalist; and my effort was rewarded on the first day of the following month—a very glorious day it was for me—by a letter from an editor containing a cheque for one pound ten shillings and sixpence. But to show you how little I deserve to be called a professional woman, how little I know of the struggles and difficulties of such lives, I have to admit that instead of spending that sum upon bread and butter, rent, shoes and stockings, or butcher's bills, I went out and bought a cat—a beautiful cat, a Persian cat, which very soon involved me in bitter disputes with my neighbours.

作家不需要钢琴和模特，也无须去巴黎、维也纳和柏林，更不用请教师。当然，纸张的廉价才是女性相较于其他职业先在写作上取得成功的原因。

还是和你们讲讲我的故事吧——很简单。你们只需想象卧室里有一个女孩，手里握着一支笔。她只需要不断地将笔从左移到右——从10点写到1点。然后，她想到一件简单又不费钱的事——把那几页纸撕下来塞进信封，在信封一角贴上一张一便士邮票，再把它丢进街角的红色邮箱里。就这样，我成了一名新闻工作者；我的努力在次月的第一天得到了回报——对我来说那是非常光荣的一天——一位编辑来信，信里有一张一英镑十先令六便士的支票。但为了让你们知道我是多么不配被称作一名职业女性，我对这类生活的挣扎与艰辛了解得有多么少，我必须承认，我没有把这笔钱花在面包、黄油、房租、鞋袜或买肉上，而是去买了一只猫——一只很漂亮的波斯猫，它很快就把我卷入了和邻里痛苦的纠纷中。

What could be easier than to write articles and to buy Persian cats with the profits? But wait a moment. Articles have to be about something. Mine, I seem to remember, was about a novel by a famous man. And while I was writing this review, I discovered that if I were going to review books, I should need to do battle with a certain phantom. And the phantom was a woman, and when I came to know her better, I called her after the heroine of a famous poem, *The Angel in the House*. It was she who used to come between me and my paper when I was writing reviews. It was she who bothered me and wasted my time and so tormented me that at last I killed her. You who come of a younger and happier generation may not have heard of her—you may not know what I mean by the Angel in the House. I will describe her as shortly as I can. She was intensely sympathetic. She was immensely charming. She was utterly unselfish. She excelled in the difficult arts of family life. She sacrificed herself daily. If there was chicken, she took the leg; if there was a draught, she sat in it—in short she was so constituted that she never had a mind or a wish of her own, but preferred to sympathise always with the minds and wishes of others. Above all—I need not say it—she was pure. Her purity was supposed to be her chief beauty—her blushes, her great grace. In those days—the last of Queen Victoria—every house had its Angel.

写写文章，然后用稿费买几只波斯猫，还有什么比这更简单的事情呢？但是等一下。文章总得有个主题。我记得我的文章好像是和一位男性名人的小说有关。在写书评时，我发现，如果我想继续评论这本书，我需要与一只幽灵作斗争。这只幽灵是女人，当我对她有了更深入的了解后，便用一首名诗里女主人公的名字为她命名——"家庭天使"。就是她，常常在我写书评时于我和纸之间挑拨离间。就是她，扰乱我，浪费我的时间，折磨我，所以最后我杀了她。你们属于年轻幸福的一代，可能没听说过她——可能也不知道我这里提"家庭天使"是什么意思。我会尽量简短地向大家介绍一下她。她极为善解人意，魅力十足，大公无私，擅长处理家庭生活中的难题，每天都在自我牺牲。如果有鸡肉，她会选鸡腿吃；如果屋内有穿堂风，她会坐在风口——简而言之，她就是这样一种性格，从不考虑自己，也无所求，更喜欢同情他人，为他人着想。总之——无须多说——她很单纯。她的单纯本应是她最重要的美之所在——她面颊绯红，举止优雅。当时——维多利亚女王执政后期——每家都有天使。

And when I came to write, I encountered her with the very first words. The shadow of her wings fell on my page; I heard the rustling of her skirts in the room. Directly, that is to say, I took my pen in my hand to review that novel by a famous man, she slipped behind me and whispered: "My dear, you are a young woman. You are writing about a book that has been written by a man. Be sympathetic; be tender; flatter; deceive; use all the arts and wiles of our sex. Never let anybody guess that you have a mind of your own. Above all, be pure." And she made as if to guide my pen. I now record the one act for which I take some credit to myself, though the credit rightly belongs to some excellent ancestors of mine who left me a certain sum of money—shall we say five hundred pounds a year?—so that it was not necessary for me to depend solely on charm for my living. I turned upon her and caught her by the throat. I did my best to kill her. My excuse, if I were to be had up in a court of law, would be that I acted in self-defence. Had I not killed her, she would have killed me. She would have plucked the heart out of my writing. For, as I found, directly I put pen to paper, you cannot review even a novel without having a mind of your own, without expressing what you think to be the truth about human relations, morality, sex.

每当我开始写作，总会在开头几句就遇上她。她挥着翅膀的影子投在纸上，我听到她的裙摆在房间里沙沙作响。也就是说，我一拿起笔给那位男性名家的小说写书评，她就溜到我身后，低声耳语："亲爱的，你年纪尚轻，还是个女人。你在评论的是一个男人写的小说。赞成他；要温柔；恭维些；说谎话；用上我们女人所有的心计和花招。绝不能让任何人认为你有自己的思想。最重要的是看上去要单纯。"她像是要操纵我的笔。现在，我要说一件多少能归功于我自己的事情，虽然真正有功的是我那些伟大的祖先们，他们给我留了一笔财产——大概一年五百英镑吧——这样我就不必仅靠女性魅力维持生计。我发起进攻，扼住她的咽喉，尽全力杀了她。如果因此上了法庭，我也可以说我是在自卫；若我不杀了她，她就会杀了我。她会把我写作的精华剔除。因为我一动笔写作就发现，如果没有自己的思想，不能表达自己对人际关系、道德和性的真实想法，那么你连一部小说都评析不了。

And all these questions, according to the Angel of the House, cannot be dealt with freely and openly by women; they must charm, they must conciliate, they must—to put it bluntly—tell lies if they are to succeed. Thus, whenever I felt the shadow of her wing or the radiance of her halo upon my page, I took up the inkpot and flung it at her. She died hard. Her fictitious nature was of great assistance to her. It is far harder to kill a phantom than a reality. She was always creeping back when I thought I had despatched her. Though I flatter myself that I killed her in the end, the struggle was severe; it took much time that had better have been spent upon learning Greek grammar, or in roaming the world in search of adventures. But it was a real experience; it was an experience that was bound to befall all women writers at that time. Killing the Angel in the House was part of the occupation of a woman writer.

...

But to continue the story of my professional experiences. I made one pound ten and six by my first review; and I bought a Persian cat with the proceeds. Then I grew ambitious. A Persian cat is all very well, I said; but a Persian cat is not enough. I must have a motor car.

所有这些问题，按"家庭天使"的想法，女性都不能自由、公开地讨论；她们必须利用自身魅力，必须安抚，必须——坦白讲——撒谎，要想成功就得这样。于是，每当我在纸上注意到她翅膀的影子或她的光晕时，便会拿起墨水瓶猛地砸向她。杀死她可不容易。虚幻的本性给了她莫大的帮助。杀死一只幽灵比杀死一个实物难多了。每次我都以为已经解决了她，但她总能不知不觉地溜回来。尽管我安慰自己最终还是杀死了她，但搏斗很激烈；这花了我太长时间，还不如花这些时间学习希腊语语法，或遨游世界去冒险。但这是真实的经历；这种经历在当时注定会发生在每位女性作家的身上。杀死"家庭天使"也是女性作家职业生涯的一部分。

继续讲我的职业经历。第一次写的书评报酬是一英镑十先令六便士；我用这笔报酬买了只波斯猫。然后我雄心见长。我想，一只波斯猫确实不错；但有波斯猫还不够。我得有辆汽车。

And it was thus that I became a novelist—for it is a very strange thing that people will give you a motor car if you will tell them a story. It is a still stranger thing that there is nothing so delightful in the world as telling stories. It is far pleasanter than writing reviews of famous novels. And yet, if I am to obey your secretary and tell you my professional experiences as a novelist, I must tell you about a very strange experience that befell me as a novelist. And to understand it you must try first to imagine a novelist's state of mind. I hope I am not giving away professional secrets if I say that a novelist's chief desire is to be as unconscious as possible. He has to induce in himself a state of perpetual lethargy. He wants life to proceed with the utmost quiet and regularity. He wants to see the same faces, to read the same books, to do the same things day after day, month after month, while he is writing, so that nothing may break the illusion in which he is living—so that nothing may disturb or disquiet the mysterious nosings about, feelings round, darts, dashes and sudden discoveries of that very shy and illusive spirit, the imagination. I suspect that this state is the same both for men and women. Be that as it may, I want you to imagine me writing a novel in a state of trance. I want you to figure to yourselves a girl sitting with a pen in her hand, which for minutes, and indeed for hours, she never dips into the inkpot.

于是，我成了一名小说家——说来奇怪，你给人们讲个故事，他们就送你一辆汽车。更奇怪的是，世上没有比讲故事更令人开心的了。这远比为名作写书评快乐得多。不过，若按你们秘书的意思，讲讲我作为小说家的职业经历，那我必须和你们讲一件发生在我身上的很奇怪的事。要理解它，你们首先要试着想象一个小说家的精神状态。如果我说小说家最渴望的就是尽可能地保持无意识状态，希望这没有泄露职业秘密。他得尽量让自己始终保持一种慵懒的状态。他希望日子过得极其平静而规律。他希望在写作时，日复一日，月复一月，都见同样的面孔，读同样的书，做同样的事，这样就没有什么能打破他的生活幻境，这样就没有什么能惊扰那个非常羞怯的虚幻精灵——"想象力"的神秘探知和感触，以及其奔涌和猛冲，或其突然发现。我猜，这种状态男女作家都一样。不管怎样，我希望你们想象我在一种恍惚的状态下写小说。你们可以想象，一个女孩坐在那里，手中拿着一支笔，几分钟——其实是几个小时——不蘸一滴墨。

The image that comes to my mind when I think of this girl is the image of a fisherman lying sunk in dreams on the verge of a deep lake with a rod held out over the water. She was letting her imagination sweep unchecked round every rock and cranny of the world that lies submerged in the depths of our unconscious being.

...

Outwardly, what is simpler than to write books? Outwardly, what obstacles are there for a woman rather than for a man? Inwardly, I think, the case is very different; she has still many ghosts to fight, many prejudices to overcome. Indeed it will be a long time still, I think, before a woman can sit down to write a book without finding a phantom to be slain, a rock to be dashed against. And if this is so in literature, the freest of all professions for women, how is it in the new professions which you are now for the first time entering?

Those are the questions that I should like, had I time, to ask you. And indeed, if I have laid stress upon these professional experiences of mine, it is because I believe that they are, though in different forms, yours also. Even when the path is nominally open—when there is nothing to prevent a woman from being a doctor, a lawyer, a civil servant—there are many phantoms and obstacles, as I believe,

我在想象这个女孩时，脑海中浮现的画面是一个渔夫躺在深不见底的湖边，正沉浸在梦境中，手中的钓竿悬在水面上。她让自己的想象力无拘无束地掠过浸在我们潜意识深处的每块礁石、每处罅隙。

......

从表面上看，什么比著书更简单呢？从表面上看，什么障碍只针对女性而非男性呢？我认为，在内心深处，情况还是很不一样的；女性仍要和许多幽灵作斗争，仍有许多偏见要克服。事实上，我觉得女性想实现能坐下来写书而不用去斩杀幽灵或者击碎礁岩般的障碍，还需要很长时间。如果在文学——这个所有职业中对女性而言最自由的职业——中尚且如此，那么你们首次迈入的新职业又会是什么样呢？

如果有时间，这些问题是我想要问你们的。诚然，我之所以强调自己的职业经历，是因为我认为你们的职业经历也会如此，只是形式不同罢了。即使这条道路在名义上是开放的——没有什么能阻止一名女性成为医生、律师、公务员——但我相信，前路仍会有许多幽灵和障碍

looming in her way. To discuss and define them is I think of great value and importance; for thus only can the labour be shared, the difficulties be solved. But besides this, it is necessary also to discuss the ends and the aims for which we are fighting, for which we are doing battle with these formidable obstacles. Those aims cannot be taken for granted; they must be perpetually questioned and examined. The whole position, as I see it—here in this hall surrounded by women practising for the first time in history I know not how many different professions—is one of extraordinary interest and importance. You have won rooms of your own in the house hitherto exclusively owned by men. You are able, though not without great labour and effort, to pay the rent. You are earning your five hundred pounds a year. But this freedom is only a beginning—the room is your own, but it is still bare. It has to be furnished; it has to be decorated; it has to be shared. How are you going to furnish it, how are you going to decorate it? With whom are you going to share it, and upon what terms? These, I think are questions of the utmost importance and interest. For the first time in history you are able to ask them; for the first time you are able to decide for yourselves what the answers should be. Willingly would I stay and discuss those questions and answers—but not tonight. My time is up; and I must cease.

若隐若现。在我看来，探讨和认清这些十分重要，也极为值得；只有这样，我们才能共同努力，克服困难。但除此之外，还有必要探讨我们为之奋斗的目标，即我们为什么与这些艰巨难平的障碍作斗争。对那些目标不能想当然，须对它们不断提出质疑，加以检验。在我看来，今天这个场景趣味非凡、意义重大——有史以来，众多追求诸多不同职业的女性齐聚一堂。你们在以前男性专有的房子中赢得了自己的房间。你们能支付房租，虽然这需要付出巨大的辛劳和努力。你们每年靠自己就能挣五百英镑。但这种自由只是一个开始：你们拥有了自己的房间，但里面仍空空如也。房间得布置，得装饰，得分享。你们打算怎么布置，怎么装饰它？你们打算和谁分享，需要什么条件？我想，这些才是最重要，也是最关乎利害的问题。有史以来第一次你们能问这些问题；第一次你们能自行决定该如何回答。我很愿意留下来跟你们探讨这些问题和答案——但今晚不行了。时间到了，我必须打住了。

phantom ['fæntəm] *n.* 幽灵；幻觉
draught [drɑːft] *n.* 穿堂风；通风
wile [waɪl] *n.* 诡计
conciliate [kən'sɪlieɪt] *v.* 安抚；劝慰
despatch [dɪ'spætʃ] *v.* 迅速处理
nosing ['nəʊzɪŋ] *n.* 嗅到
slain [sleɪn] *v.* 杀死（slay 的过去分词）

## 弗吉尼亚·伍尔夫（Virginia Woolf，1882—1941）

英国意识流文学代表作家之一，著有《达洛维夫人》《到灯塔去》《海浪》《幕间》等。

# The Hollow Men

Thomas Stearns Eliot

**Mistah Kurtz—he dead.**

**A penny for the Old Guy**

**I**

We are the hollow men

We are the stuffed men

Leaning together

Headpiece fill with straw. Alas!

Our dried voices, when

We whisper together

Are quiet and meaningless

As wind in dry grass

Or rats' feet over broken glass

In our dry cellar

Shape without form, shade without colour,

Paralysed force, gesture without motion;

Those who have crossed

With direct eyes, to death's other Kingdom

# 空心人

〔英〕托马斯·斯特恩斯·艾略特 ｜ 赵萝蕤 译

**库尔茨先生——他死了**

**给老盖一个便士**

## 一

我们是空心人

我们是被填塞起来的人

彼此倚靠着

头颅装满了稻草。可叹啊！

我们干哑的嗓音，

在我们说悄悄话时

寂静而无意义

像干草地中的风

或我们那干燥的地窖中

耗子踩在碎玻璃堆上的步履

有态无形，有影无色，

力度麻木，打着手势却毫无动作；

那些已经亲眼目睹

跨进了死亡这另一个国度时

Remember us—if at all—not as lost

Violent souls, but only

As the hollow men

The stuffed men.

**II**

Eyes I dare not meet in dreams

In death's dream kingdom

These do not appear:

There, the eyes are

Sunlight on a broken column

There, is a tree swinging

And voices are

In the wind's singing

More distant and more solemn

Than a fading star.

Let me be no nearer

In death's dream kingdom

Let me also wear

Such deliberate disguises

Rat's coat, crowskin, crossed staves

只要记得我们——不是

丢魂失魄的野人，而只是

空心人

被填塞起来的人。

二

我在梦中不敢面对的眼睛

在死亡的梦乡

不会显现：

在那里，眼睛是

断柱上的阳光

在那里，一棵树在摇曳

而人声只是

在风中歌唱

比一颗正在消逝的星星

更加遥远而庄严。

不要让我挨近

死亡的梦乡

让我也穿上

这些刻意的伪装

老鼠皮，乌鸦皮，交叉杖

In a field

Behaving as the wind behaves

No nearer—

Not that final meeting

In the twilight kingdom

**III**

This is the dead land

This is cactus land

Here the stone images

Are raised, here they receive

The supplication of a dead man's hand

Under the twinkle of a fading star.

Is it like this

In death's other kingdom

Waking alone

At the hour when we are

Trembling with tenderness

Lips that would kiss

Form prayers to broken stone.

在田野里

像风一样行动

不用靠近——

不是黄昏之乡的

最后相会

三

这是死亡的地带

这是仙人掌的地带

在这里，石头的人像

被竖立起，在这里他们接受

一只死人的手的哀求

在一颗消逝的星星的闪光下。

在死亡的另一个国度里

是否这样

独自醒来

而那一刻我们正

感受着温柔的震颤

想要亲吻的双唇

形成了对破碎石头的祈祷。

## IV

The eyes are not here

There are no eyes here

In this valley of dying stars

In this hollow valley

This broken jaw of our lost kingdoms

In this last of meeting places

We grope together

and avoid speech

Gathered on this beach of the tumid river

Sightless, unless

The eyes reappear

As the perpetual star

Multifoliate rose

Of death's twilight kingdom

The hope only

Of empty men.

## V

Here we go round the prickly pear

Prickly pear, prickly pear

# 四

眼睛不在这里

在这星星即将死去的山谷

在这空心的山谷

在这已经为我们所失的破碎的王国

没有眼睛

在这最后的相会处

我们一起摸索

避免交谈

在这条涨水的河畔聚会

看不见，除非

眼睛重新出现

如同那死亡的黄昏之国的

永恒之星

重瓣的玫瑰

空心人的

唯一希望。

# 五

我们在这里围绕仙人掌转圈

仙人掌啊仙人掌

Here we go round the prickly pear
At five o'clock in the morning.

Between the idea
And the reality
Between the motion
And the act
Falls the shadow

*For Thine is the Kingdom*

Between the conception
And the creation
Between the emotion
And the response
Falls the Shadow

*Life is very long.*

Between the desire
And the spasm
Between the potency
and the existence
Between the essence
And the descent
Falls the Shadow.

我们在这里围绕仙人掌转圈

在凌晨五点。

在理想

和现实之间

在动作

和行为之间

落下帷幕

*因为王国为你所有*

在概念

和创造之间

在情感

和回应之间

落下帷幕

*生命如此漫长*

在欲望

和痉挛之间

在潜能

和生存之间

在本质

和遗传之间

落下帷幕

*For Thine is the Kingdom.*

For thine is

Life is

For Thine is the

This is the way the world ends

This is the way the world ends

This is the way the world ends

Not with a bang but a whimper.

🐦 难词释义 ·································································· •

stuffed [stʌft] *adj.* 填制的；（人）吃饱的

deliberate [dɪ'lɪbərət] *adj.* 故意的；深思熟虑的

crowskin ['krəʊˌskɪn] *n.* 乌鸦皮

cactus ['kæktəs] *n.* 仙人掌

supplication [ˌsʌplɪ'keɪʃn] *n.* 恳求；祈祷

grope [grəʊp] *v.* 摸索；探寻

tumid ['tjuːmɪd] *adj.* 肿胀的

multifoliate [ˌmʌltɪ'fəʊlɪɪt] *adj.* 多叶的

prickly ['prɪkli] *adj.* 多刺的

spasm ['spæzəm] *n.* 痉挛；抽搐

potency ['pəʊtnsi] *n.* 潜能；影响力

因为王国为你所有

因为你是

生命是

因为你就是

世界就是这样终结的

世界就是这样终结的

世界就是这样终结的

不是一声砰响，而是一声呜咽。

**托马斯·斯特恩斯·艾略特（Thomas Stearns Eliot，1888—1965）**

英国诗人、剧作家、文学评论家和编辑，著有《荒原》《四个四重奏》等作品，并于 1948 年被授予诺贝尔文学奖。从 20 世纪 20 年代到该世纪末，艾略特对英美文化产生了深远的影响。《空心人》是艾略特在 1925 年创作的作品，也是失去灵魂的现代人的象征。诗歌集中表现了西方人面对现代文明濒临崩溃、希望渺茫的困境，以及精神极为空虚的生存状态。

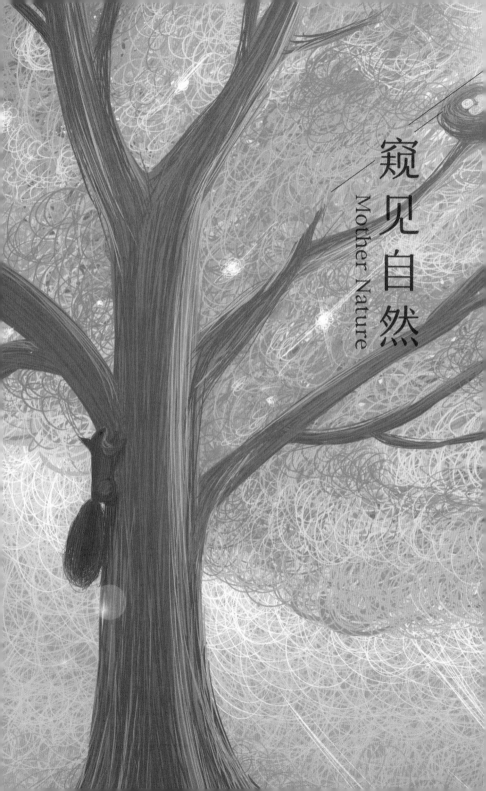

窥见自然
Mother Nature

# Hour in the Sun

John Bradley

"...I was rich, if not in money, in sunny hours and summer days."

—Henry David Thoreau

When Thoreau wrote that line, he was thinking of the Walden Pond he knew as a boy.

Woodchoppers and the Iron Horse had not yet greatly damaged the beauty of its setting. A boy could go to the pond and lie on his back against the seat of a boat, lazily drifting from shore while the loons dived and the swallows dipped around him. Thoreau loved to recall such sunny hours and summer days "when idleness was the most attractive and productive business".

I too was once a boy in love with a pond, rich in sunny hours and summer days. Sun and summer are still what they always were, but the boy and the pond changed. The boy, who is now a man, no longer finds much time for idle drifting. The pond has been annexed by a great city. The swamps where herons once hunted are now drained and filled with houses. The bay where water lilies quietly floated is now a harbor for motor boats. In short, everything that the boy loved no longer exists—except in the man's memory of it.

# 阳光下的时光

[美] 约翰·布莱德利

"……虽然我不是富甲天下，却拥有无数个艳阳天与夏日。"

——亨利·大卫·梭罗

梭罗写下这句话时，想到的是孩提时代就熟悉的瓦尔登湖。

当时伐木者和火车尚未严重破坏湖畔的美丽景致。小男孩可以走向湖边，仰卧在小舟上，自此岸缓缓漂向彼岸。周遭有潜鸟戏水，燕子翻飞。梭罗喜欢回忆这样的艳阳天和夏日，那时"慵懒是最迷人、最具生产力的事情"。

我曾经也是个热爱湖塘的小男孩，拥有无数个艳阳天与夏日。如今阳光、夏日依旧，男孩和湖塘却已改变。男孩已长大成人，不再有那么多时间泛舟湖上。而湖塘也为大城市所并。曾有苍鹭觅食的沼泽，如今已枯干殆尽，上面盖满了房舍。睡莲静静漂浮的湖湾，现在成了汽艇的港湾。总之，男孩所爱的一切都已不复存在——只留在他的回忆中。

Some people insist that only today and tomorrow matter. But how much poorer we would be if we really lived by that rule! So much of what we do today is frivolous and futile and soon forgotten. So much of what we hope to do tomorrow never happens.

The past is the bank in which we store our most valuable possession: the memories that give meaning and depth to our lives.

Those who truly treasure the past will not bemoan the passing of the good old days, because days enshrined in memory are never lost. Death itself is powerless to still a remembered voice or erase a remembered smile. And for one boy who is now a man, there is a pond which neither time nor tide can change, where he can still spend a quiet hour in the sun.

### 难词释义

loon [luːn] *n.* 潜鸟
annex ['æneks] *v.* 吞并
heron ['herən] *n.* 鹭
drain [dreɪn] *v.* 排空；（使）流光；放干
frivolous ['frɪvələs] *adj.* 可笑的；愚蠢的
futile ['fjuːtaɪl] *adj.* 徒劳的；无效的
bemoan [bɪ'məʊn] *v.* 悲叹；哀怨

有些人坚持认为只有今天和明天才是重要的，可是如果真的照此生活，我们将是何等可怜！许多今天我们所做的事是可笑又徒劳的，很快就会被忘记。许多我们期待明天要做的事却永远不会发生。

过去是一所银行，我们将最可贵的财产——记忆——珍藏其中。记忆赋予我们生命的意义和深度。

真正珍惜过去的人，不会悲叹旧日美好时光的逝去，因为珍藏于记忆中的时光永不流逝。死亡本身无法止住记忆中的声音，也不能擦除记忆中的微笑。对一个已经长大成人的男孩来说，有一个湖塘不会因时间或潮汐而改变，在那里，他可以继续享受阳光下安静的时光。

# The Edge of the Sea (Excerpts)

### Rachel Carson

The shore is an ancient world, for as long as there has been an earth and sea there has been this place of the meeting of land and water. Yet it is a world that keeps alive the sense of continuing creation and of the relentless drive of life. Each time that I enter it, I gain some new awareness of its beauty and its deeper meanings, sensing that intricate fabric of life by which one creature is linked with another, and each with its surroundings.

In my thoughts of the shore, one place stands apart for its revelation of exquisite beauty. It is a pool hidden within a cave that one can visit only rarely and briefly when the lowest of the year's low tides fall below it, and perhaps from that very fact it acquires some of its special beauty. Choosing such a tide, I hoped for a glimpse of the pool. The ebb was to fall early in the morning. I knew that if the wind held from the northwest and no interfering swell ran in from a distant storm, the level of the sea should drop below the entrance to the pool. There had been sudden ominous showers in the night, with rain like handfuls of gravel flung on the roof.

# 海之滨（节选）

[美] 蕾切尔·卡森

海岸是一个古老的世界。自从有陆地和海洋以来，就有这个水陆相接的地方。但人们却感觉，在那里创造从未停止，生命力顽强不息。每当我踏入这个世界，都会对它的美和深层意蕴产生新的认识，能够感觉到生物彼此之间以及与周围环境之间是通过错综复杂的生命结构紧密相连的。

每当我想起海岸，脑海中就会浮现一个美轮美奂、与众不同的地方。那是一汪隐匿于洞中的水潭。平时，洞被海水所淹没，一年之中只有当海潮降到低于水潭时，人们才能在这难得的时候匆匆看它一眼。也许正因如此，它被赋予了一种特殊的美。我选好这样一个低潮的时机，希望能看一眼水潭。潮水将在清晨退去。我知道，如果不刮西北风，远处的暴风雨不再掀起惊涛骇浪进行干扰，海平面就会降到水潭的入口以下。夜里突然下了几场让我感觉不妙的阵雨，雨点似一把把碎石般落在屋顶上。

When I looked out into the early morning, the sky was full of a gray dawn light but the sun had not yet risen. Water and air were pallid. Across the bay the moon was a luminous disc in the western sky, suspended above the dim line of distant shore—the full August moon, drawing the tide to the low, low levels of the threshold of the alien sea world. As I watched, a gull flew by, above the spruces. Its breast was rosy with the light of the unrisen sun. The day was, after all, to be fair.

Later, as I stood above the tide near the entrance to the pool, the promise of that rosy light was sustained. From the base of the steep wall of rock on which I stood, a moss-covered ledge jutted seaward into deep water. In the surge at the rim of the ledge the dark fronds of oarweeds swayed, smooth and gleaming as leather. The projecting ledge was the path to the small hidden cave and its pool. Occasionally a swell, stronger than the rest, rolled smoothly over the rim and broke in foam against the cliff. But the intervals between such swells were long enough to admit me to the ledge and long enough for a glimpse of that fairy pool, so seldom and so briefly exposed.

And so I knelt on the wet carpet of sea moss and looked back into the dark cavern that held the pool in a shallow basin.

清晨，我向外眺望，天空中透着灰蒙蒙的曙光，但是太阳还没有升起。海水和天空一片暗淡。一轮明月挂在海湾对面的西天上，远方的海岸变成了月下灰暗的线条——八月的望月把潮水吸得很低，使得那片与人世隔绝的海洋世界之门隐约可见。就在我观望的时候，一只海鸥飞过云杉林。呼之欲出的太阳把它的腹部照得红彤彤的。终于，天放晴了。

后来，当我站在高于海潮的水潭入口处附近时，天空依然透着瑰红色的霞光。在我立足的峭岩底部，有一块长满青苔的礁石伸向大海最深处。海水拍击着礁石边缘，水藻上下左右地飘动，像皮面般滑溜发亮。那块凸出的礁石正是通往隐蔽的洞穴和水潭的路径。偶尔会有一个大浪平稳地越过礁石的边缘拍打在岩壁上，击出水沫。但这些大浪之间的间隔足以让我踏上礁石，看一眼那汪鲜少露面、短暂揭去面纱的仙洞水潭。

我弯膝跪在湿漉漉的苔藓地毯上，转过头探看黑暗的洞穴。洞穴里的水潭很浅，

The floor of the cave was only a few inches below the roof, and a mirror had been created in which all that grew on the ceiling was reflected in the still water below.

Under water that was clear as glass the pool was carpeted with green sponge. Gray patches of sea squirts glistened on the ceiling and colonies of soft coral were a pale apricot color. In the moment when I looked into the cave, a little elfin starfish hung down, suspended by the merest thread, perhaps by only a single tube foot. It reached down to touch its own reflection, so perfectly delineated that there might have been, not one starfish, but two. The beauty of the reflected images and of the limpid pool itself was the poignant beauty of things that are ephemeral, existing only until the sea should return to fill the little cave.

📌 难词释义

pallid ['pælɪd] *adj.* 苍白的；暗淡的
jut [dʒʌt] *v.* 突出；伸出
ledge [ledʒ] *n.* 岩脊；岩架
cavern ['kævən] *n.* 大洞穴
apricot ['eɪprɪkɒt] *n.* 杏黄色
elfin ['elfɪn] *adj.* 小巧玲珑的
limpid ['lɪmpɪd] *adj.* 清澈的

洞穴的底部距离顶部只有几英寸高。真是一面天造明镜！洞顶上长着的生物都倒映在下方平静的水面上。

清明如镜的水底遍布碧绿的海绵。洞顶上一片片灰色的海鞘闪闪发光，一簇簇软珊瑚披着淡淡的杏黄色衣裳。就在我朝洞里探望时，发现一只小海星挂在上面，仅凭一根线吊着身体，或许那是它的一只管足。它向下触碰自己的倒影。那倒影真是栩栩如生，仿佛不止有一只海星，而是两只。水中倒影的美和清澈的水潭本身的美，都是转瞬即逝的事物身上自带的凄美——海水一旦漫过洞穴，这种美便不复存在了。

蕾切尔·卡森（Rachel Carson，1907—1964）

美国生物学家，以其关于环境污染和海洋自然历史的著作而闻名，包括《我们周围的海洋》《海洋的边缘》《寂静的春天》等。其中，《寂静的春天》被看作激起全世界环境保护事业的开山之作。

# A Fish of the World

Terry Jones

Herring once decided to swim right around the world. "I'm tired of the North Sea," he said. "I want to find out what else there is in the world." So he swam off south into the deep Atlantic. He swam and swam far, far away from the seas he knew, through the warm waters of the equator and on down into the south Atlantic. And all the time he saw many strange and wonderful fish that he had never seen before. Once he was nearly eaten by a shark. And once he was nearly electrocuted by an electric eel. And once he was nearly stung by a stingray.

But he swam on and on. Round the tip of Africa and into the Indian Ocean, and he passed by devilfish and sailfish and sawfish and swordfish and bluefish and blackfish and mudfish and some fish, and he was amazed by the different shapes and sizes and colours. On he swam into the Java Sea. And he saw fish that leapt out of the water and fish that lived on the bottom of the sea and fish that could walk on their fins. And on he swam through the Coral Sea where the shells of millions and millions of tiny creatures had turned to rock and stood as big as mountains.

# 无所不知的鱼

[英] 特里·琼斯

从前，有一条鲱鱼决心要环游世界。"我已经厌倦了北海，"他说，"我想知道世界其他地方有些什么东西。"于是他向南游向了大西洋深处。他游啊游，远离他熟悉的海洋，穿过赤道附近温暖的水域，一直游到南大西洋。一路上，他看到了许多以前从未见过的稀奇古怪的鱼。有一次，他差点被鲨鱼吃掉；还有一次，他差点被电鳗电死；又有一次，他差点被黄貂鱼刺伤。

可他还是继续不停地往前游，绕过非洲最南端，进入印度洋。形形色色的鱼从他身边游过，有魔鬼鱼、旗鱼、锯鳐、箭鱼、蓝鱼、黑鲸、泥鱼，等等，他对这些鱼的不同形状、大小和颜色感到诧异。接着，他游进了爪哇海，看到了能跃出水面的鱼、生活在海底的鱼和能用鳍行走的鱼。再接着，他游到了珊瑚海，在那里，数百万微小生物的壳变成了岩石，堆积如山。

But still he swam on into the wide Pacific. He swam over the deepest parts of the ocean where the water is so deep that it is inky black at the bottom and the fish carried lanterns over their heads and some have lights on their tails. And through the Pacific he swam and then he turned north and headed up to the cold Siberian Sea where huge white icebergs sailed past him like mighty ships, and still he swam on and on and into the frozen Arctic Ocean where the sea is forever covered in ice. And on he went past Greenland and Iceland and finally he swam home into his own North Sea.

All his friends and relations gathered around and made a great fuss of him. They had a big feast and offered him the very best food they could find, but the herring just yawned and said, "I've swum around the entire world. I've seen everything there is to see and I have eaten more exotic and wonderful dishes than you could possibly imagine." And he refused to eat anything. Then his friends and relations begged him to come home and live with them. But he refused. "I've been everywhere there is and that old rock is too dull and small for me." And he went off and lived on his own.

但他仍然继续向广阔的太平洋游去。他游到了太平洋的最深处，那里的水很深，海底一片漆黑，有些鱼的头上举着灯笼，有些鱼的尾巴上点着灯。穿过太平洋，他向北游往寒冷的西伯利亚海，在那里，巨大的白色冰山像一艘艘巨轮从他身边驶过。他继续游啊游，游到了冰封的北冰洋，那里的海常年被冰块覆盖。接着，他游过了格陵兰岛和冰岛，最后游回了他的老家——北海。

他的亲戚朋友全都来了，围着他问长问短。他们设宴款待他，把他们能找到的最好的食物端出来请他品尝，可鲱鱼只是打了个哈欠，说："我已经游遍了整个世界，见识过了世界上所有的东西。我尝过的奇珍异馐多得超出你们的想象。"他什么都没吃。后来，他的亲戚朋友恳求他回家和他们同住，但他拒绝了。"我哪儿都去过了，那块烂礁石又暗又小，简直没法住。"说完他就走了，独自生活。

And when the breeding season came, he refused to join in the spawning, saying, "I've swum around the entire world. And now I know how many fish there are in the world. I can't be interested in herrings anymore."

Eventually, one of the oldest of the herrings swam up to him and said, "Listen, if you don't spawn with us, some herrings eggs will go unfertilised and will not turn into healthy young herrings. If you don't live with your family, you'll make them sad and if you don't eat, you'll die."

But the herring said, "I don't mind. I've been everywhere there is to go, I've seen everything there is to see, and now I know everything there is to know."

The old fish shook his head. "No one has ever seen everything there is to see," he said. "Nor known everything there is to know."

"Look," said the herring, "I've swum through the North Sea, the Atlantic Ocean, the Indian Ocean, the Java Sea, the Coral Sea, the Great Pacific Ocean, the Siberian Sea, and the frozen Arctic. Tell me, what else is there for me to see or know?"

"I don't know," said the old herring. "But there may be something."

当繁殖季节来临时，他拒绝参与产卵，还说："我游遍了全世界。现在我知道世界上有多少种鱼了。我不可能再对鲱鱼感兴趣了。"

最后，一条年长的鲱鱼游到他面前对他说："听着，如果你不和我们一起参与产卵，有些鲱鱼卵就不能受精，无法变成健康的小鲱鱼。如果你不和你的家人住在一起，会让他们伤心。还有，如果你不吃东西，会没命的。"

可是鲱鱼说："我不在乎。能去的地方我都去过了，能见到的东西我也都见过了，现在，我已经无所不知了。"

老鲱鱼摇了摇头，说："没有人能看遍世界上所有的东西，也没有人能无所不知。"

"你看，"鲱鱼说，"我游过了北海、大西洋、印度洋、爪哇海、珊瑚海、太平洋、西伯利亚海，甚至冰天雪地的北冰洋。你告诉我，还有什么是我要看到或要知道的？"

"我不知道，"老鲱鱼说，"不过总会有些东西是你没见过或不知道的。"

Well, just then, a fishing boat came by, and all the herrings were caught in a net and taken to market that very day. And a man bought the herring and ate it for his supper, and he never knew that it had swum right around the world and had seen everything there was to see, and knew everything there was to know.

🐟 难词释义 ························································· •

herring ['herɪŋ] *n.* 鲱鱼
electrocute [ɪ'lektrəkjuːt] *v.* 使触电受伤
stingray ['stɪŋreɪ] *n.* 黄貂鱼
devilfish ['devəlˌfɪʃ] *n.* 魔鬼鱼；蝠鲼
sailfish ['seɪlfɪʃ] *n.* 旗鱼
sawfish ['sɔːˌfɪʃ] *n.* 锯鳐
spawn [spɔːn] *v.* 产卵

正在这时，一条捕鱼船开了过来，所有的鲱鱼被一网打尽，当天就被送到了市场。一个人买走了那条鲱鱼，做成了晚餐。这个人永远也不会知道他吃掉的这条鲱鱼曾经环游过世界，见识过世界上的一切，对世界上的东西无所不知。

特里·琼斯（Terry Jones，1942—2020）

英国导演、喜剧演员、剧作家，主要作品有《巨蟒剧团之飞翔的马戏团》《小鱼历险记》《撒谎精自传》等。

# Nature (Excerpts)

Ralph Waldo Emerson

To speak truly, few adult persons can see nature. Most persons do not see the sun. At least they have a very superficial seeing. The sun illuminates only the eye of the man, but shines into the eye and the heart of the child. The lover of nature is he whose inward and outward senses are still truly adjusted to each other; who has retained the spirit of infancy even into the era of manhood. His intercourse with heaven and earth, becomes part of his daily food. In the presence of nature, a wild delight runs through the man, in spite of real sorrows. Nature says, he is my creature, and maugre all his impertinent griefs, he shall be glad with me. Not the sun or the summer alone, but every hour and season yields its tribute of delight; for every hour and change corresponds to and authorises a different state of the mind, from breathless noon to grimmest midnight. Nature is a setting that fits equally well a comic or a mourning piece. In good health, the air is a cordial of incredible virtue. Crossing a bare common, in snow puddles, at twilight, under a clouded sky, without having in my thoughts any occurrence of special good fortune, I have enjoyed a perfect exhilaration. I am glad to the brink of fear.

# 论自然（节选）

[美]拉尔夫·瓦尔多·爱默生 ｜ 唐根金 译

说实话，很少有成年人能真正看见自然。大多数人都不会去看太阳，即便看，最多也只是一瞥而过。对成年人而言，阳光只是照亮了他的眼睛，但对孩子而言，阳光却能透过眼睛照进孩子的心灵。一个真正热爱自然的人，外在的知觉和内心的感触是合二为一的，即使在他长大成人以后，仍保持着童心未泯。对他来说，与天地的交流是日常生活中不可或缺的一部分。面对大自然，哪怕生活中有再大的忧伤，他的内心也会涌起莫大的喜悦。大自然说，他是我的造物，尽管他有各种忧伤，但与我一起时他将获得快乐。自然带给我们的不单单是阳光和夏日，每个时辰、每个季节，她还给我们带来欢乐和欣喜。从沉闷的中午到漆黑的午夜，自然变化的每一时辰无不如是，都意味着一种全新的心境。在自然这个大舞台上，既能上演喜剧，也能烘托悲情。如果身心健康，那么，你会觉得空气也犹如美妙的甜饮。当我在黎明阴沉的天空下踏着积雪的水坑，穿过空旷的公地时，虽然明知道不会有什么特别的好运降临，内心仍感到无比愉悦，以致有些胆怯。

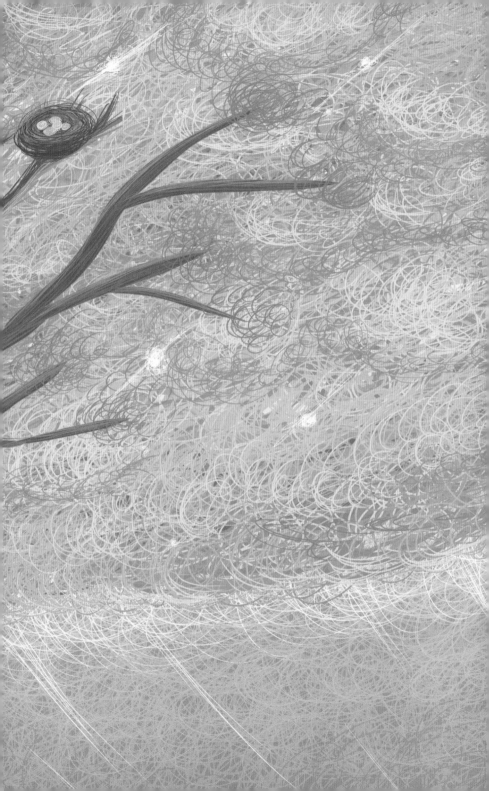

In the woods too, a man casts off his years, as the snake his slough, and at what period soever of life, is always a child. In the woods, is perpetual youth. Within these plantations of God, a decorum and sanctity reign, a perennial festival is dressed, and the guest sees not how he should tire of them in a thousand years. In the woods, we return to reason and faith. There I feel that nothing can befall me in life, no disgrace, no calamity, (leaving me my eyes) which nature cannot repair. Standing on the bare ground, my head bathed by the blithe air, and uplifted into infinite space, all mean egotism vanishes. I become a transparent eyeball; I am nothing; I see all; the currents of the universal being circulate through me; I am part or particle of God. In the tranquil landscape, and especially in the distant line of the horizon, man beholds somewhat as beautiful as his own nature.

🐬 难词释义 ············································································· •

maugre ['mɔːɡə] *prep.* 尽管
cordial ['kɔːdiəl] *n.* （不含酒精、加水饮用的）甜果汁饮料
common ['kɒmən] *n.* 公共用地
slough [slʌf] *n.* （蛇等）蜕下的皮
decorum [dɪ'kɔːrəm] *n.* 礼貌得体；端庄稳重
sanctity ['sæŋktəti] *n.* 圣洁；神圣不可侵犯性
perennial [pə'reniəl] *adj.* 长久的；持续的
blithe [blaɪð] *adj.* 快乐的；无忧无虑的

在森林中也是如此，人褪下岁月的痕迹，就如同蛇蜕去身上的皮，无论身处生命的哪个阶段，永远心如孩童。在森林里，青春永恒。在这些上帝掌管的园地里，礼仪与圣洁统治着一切，庆典四季不断，客人沉醉其中，千年不倦。在森林里，我们回归理性和信仰。在那里，任何不幸都不会降临在我的身上，没有什么耻辱、灾难（除非我的眼睛看不见）是自然无法平复的。当我驻足旷野，任由思绪飘荡在宜人的空气中向上无限升腾，一切卑劣的私心杂念都荡然无存。我变成了一颗透明的眼球，渺小至极，却洞悉一切。世间生灵汇成一股洪流，在我周身环绕，我成了上帝的一部分。在静谧的风景里，尤其是在那遥远的地平线上，人们看见了某种与他本性一般美好的事物。

拉尔夫·瓦尔多·爱默生（Ralph Waldo Emerson，1803—1882）

美国著名思想家、文学家和诗人，超验主义哲学的代表人，美国前总统林肯称其为"美国的孔子"。《论自然》被认为是超验主义哲学思想的宣言。

# August (Excerpts)

Charles Dickens

There is no month in the whole year, in which nature wears a more beautiful appearance than in the month of August.

Spring has many beauties, and May is a fresh and blooming month, but the charms of this time of year are enhanced by their contrast with the winter season.

August has no such advantage.

It comes when we remember nothing but clear skies, green fields, and sweet-smelling flowers—when the recollection of snow, and ice, and bleak winds, has faded from our minds as completely as they have disappeared from the earth—and yet what a pleasant time it is!

Orchards and cornfields ring with the hum of labours; trees bend beneath the thick clusters of rich fruit which bow their branches to the ground; and the corn, piled in graceful sheaves, or waving in every light breath that sweeps above it, as if it wooed the sickle, tinges the landscape with a golden hue.

# 八月之美（节选）

[英] 查尔斯·狄更斯

一年之中，没有任何一个月份的自然风光比得过八月的风采。

春天美不胜收，五月清新明媚、繁花似锦，但这些时节的魅力是通过与冬天的对比而增强的。

八月没有这样的优势。

它来的时候，我们脑海中都是明朗的天空、碧绿的田野，还有芳香四溢的花朵——至于冰雪和刺骨的寒风，则完全被抛之脑后，仿佛它们已经从地球上消失了一样——然而八月是一个多么令人惬意的季节啊！

果园和麦田到处都充溢着忙碌劳作的声音；串串果实压得果树弯下了腰，枝条低垂到地上；麦子或是优雅地一捆捆堆挤在一起，或是迎风招展，仿佛在向镰刀求爱，给周围的景致染上了一层金黄的色调。

A mellow softness appears to hang over the whole earth; the influence of the season seems to extend itself to the very wagon, whose slow motion across the well-reaped field, is perceptible only to the eye, but strikes with no harsh sound upon the ear.

🐬 难词释义 ...............................................................

recollection [ˌrekə'lekʃn] *n.* 回忆；往事
sheaf [ʃiːf] *n.* 捆；束；扎
woo [wuː] *v.* 追求；恳求
sickle ['sɪkl] *n.* 镰刀
tinge [tɪndʒ] *v.* 微染
mellow ['meləʊ] *adj.* 柔和的；悦耳的
perceptible [pə'septəbl] *adj.* 可察觉的；看得见的

整个大地似乎笼罩在一种醇香柔和的气氛中；就连马车也难免受此时节的影响，只有眼睛才能察觉到它们缓慢穿过收割好的田地，耳旁却寂静无声。

**查尔斯·狄更斯（Charles Dickens，1812—1870）**

英国小说家，作品良多，1837 年完成的第一部长篇小说《匹克威克外传》奠定了其在英国文学界的地位。代表作有《雾都孤儿》《老古玩店》《远大前程》《大卫·科波菲尔》《艰难时世》《双城记》等。

# Night

Nathaniel Hawthorne

Night has fallen over the country. Through the trees rises the red moon and the stars are scarcely seen. In the vast shadow of night the coolness and the dews descend. I sit at the open window to enjoy them; and hear only the voice of the summer wind. Like black hulks, the shadows of the great trees ride at anchor on the billowy sea of grass. I cannot see the red and blue flowers, but I know that they are there. Far away in the meadow gleams the silver Charles. The tramp of horses' hoofs sounds from the wooden bridge. Then all is still save the continuous wind of the summer night. Sometimes I know not if it be the wind or the sound of the neighboring sea. The village clock strikes; and I feel that I am not alone.

How different it is in the city! It is late, and the crowd is gone. You step out upon the balcony, and lie in the very bosom of the cool, dewy night as if you folded her garments about you. Beneath lies the public walk with trees, like a fathomless, black gulf, into whose silent darkness the spirit plunges, and float away with some beloved spirit clasped in its embrace. The lamps are still burning up and down the long street.

# 夜

[美]纳撒尼尔·霍桑

夜幕降临，笼罩着乡间。一轮红月正从树林边升起，天上几乎看不到星星。夜色苍茫，寒气与露水渐渐显现。我坐在窗前欣赏夜色，窗户开着，耳边只能听到夏天的风声。大树的影子像黑色的巨轮，停泊在波浪起伏的茫茫草海上。虽然我看不见红色和蓝色的花，但我知道，它们就在那里。远处的草地上，银色的查尔斯河闪闪发光。木桥那边传来沉重的马蹄声。接着，万物俱寂，只留下夏夜不绝的风声。有时，我分辨不出那究竟是风声，还是邻近的海涛声。这时候，村子里的钟敲响了，我才觉得我并不孤单。

城市的夜晚是多么不同啊！夜深人散，你走上阳台，躺在露水浸润的凉爽夜幕中，仿佛将这夜色作为外衣裹在了身上。阳台下面的人行道上，树木繁茂，像一条深不可测的黑色海湾，飘忽的精灵就这样跳进寂静的黑暗中，拥抱着某个心爱的精灵随波荡漾而去了。长街上的灯依然亮着。

People go by with grotesque shadows, now foreshortened, and now lengthening away into the darkness and vanishing, while a new one springs up behind the walker, and seems to pass him revolving like the sail of a windmill. The iron gates of the park shut with a jangling clang. There are footsteps and loud voices;—a tumult; —a drunken brawl; —an alarm of fire;—then silence again. And now at length the city is asleep, and we can see the night. The belated moon looks over the roofs, and finds no one to welcome her. The moonlight is broken. It lies here and there in the squares and the opening of the streets—angular like blocks of white marble.

 难词释义

hulk [hʌlk] *n.* 大块头，庞然大物
billowy ['bɪləʊi] *adj.* 汹涌的；巨浪似的
hoof [huːf] *n.* （马等动物的）蹄；人的脚
fathomless ['fæðəmləs] *adj.* 深不可测的
foreshorten [fɔːˈʃɔːtn] *v.* 缩短
jangle ['dʒæŋgl] *v.* 使发出刺耳声
clang [klæŋ] *n.* 叮当声；铿锵声
tumult ['tjuːmʌlt] *n.* 喧哗；骚动
brawl [brɔːl] *n.* 斗殴；闹事

人们从灯下走过，拖拽着各种各样奇形怪状的影子，时而缩短，时而拉长，不一会儿的工夫，就消失在了黑暗中。但当有行人走过路灯的一刹那，新的影子又会突然出现，像风车上的翼板一样，"呼"地从后方转到那人前方去。公园的铁门哐当一声关上，耳边传来脚步声和响亮的说话声，然后是喧闹声、醉酒后的吵嚷声、火警声。接着，又寂静如初。现在，这座城市终于睡着了，我们可以观看夜色了。姗姗来迟的月亮从屋顶后方探出脸来，发现没有人欢迎她。于是月光碎了一地，洒落在各个广场和宽阔的大街上，棱角分明，像一块块白色的大理石。

纳撒尼尔·霍桑（Nathaniel Hawthorne，1804—1864）

美国小说家，其代表作包括长篇小说《红字》《七角楼》，短篇小说集《重讲一遍的故事》《古屋青苔》《雪影》等。其中《红字》为世界文学经典，被认为是美国最好的小说之一。

# The Dew Drop

Peter Hughes

As the sun rose, a dew drop became aware of its surroundings. There it sat on a leaf, catching the sunlight and throwing it back out. Proud of its simple beauty, it was very content. Around it were other dew drops, some on the same leaf and some on other leaves round about. The dew drop was sure that it was the best, the most special dew drop of them all.

Ah, it was good to be a dew drop.

The wind rose and the plant began to shake, tipping the leaf. Terror gripped the dew drop as gravity pulled it towards the edge of the leaf, towards the unknown. Why? Why was this happening? Things were comfortable. Things were safe. Why did they have to change? Why? Why?

The dew drop reached the edge of the leaf. It was terrified, certain that it would be smashed into a thousand pieces below, sure that this was the end. The day had only just begun and the end had come so quickly. It seemed so unfair. It seemed so meaningless. It tried desperately to do whatever it could to cling to the leaf, but it was no use.

# 一颗露珠

[美] 彼得·休斯

当太阳升起时，一颗露珠苏醒过来。它坐在一片叶子上，一边捕捉阳光，一边又将其反射出去。它美得那样纯粹，不禁有些沾沾自喜。在它的周围，还有许多其他的露珠，它们有的和它在同一片叶子上，有的在其他叶子上。但是露珠相信，自己是最棒、最特别的那一颗。

啊，当一颗露珠真好！

起风了，植物开始摇晃，叶子也开始倾倒。重力将露珠拉向叶子边缘，拉向未知，恐惧随之降临。为什么？为什么会这样呢？从前是多么舒适，多么安全，为什么变成现在这样了？为什么？为什么？

露珠滑落到叶子边缘。它惊恐万分，坚信自己一旦掉下去，必将粉身碎骨，然后一切都完了。这一天明明才刚刚开始，怎么这么快就要结束？太不公平了！真是白忙活一场！露珠拼命地想抓住叶子，但是无济于事。

Finally, it let go, surrendering to the pull of gravity. Down, down it fell. Below there seemed to be a mirror. A reflection of itself seemed to be coming up to meet the dew drop. Closer and closer they came together until finally...

And then the fear transformed into deep joy as the tiny dew drop merged with the vastness that was the pond. Now the dew drop was no more, but it was not destroyed.

It had become one with the whole.

### 难词释义

tip [tɪp] v. （使）倾斜，（使）斜倒
grip [grɪp] v. 紧握；紧抓

终于，它放弃了，向重力屈服。它往下滚啊滚。下面似乎有一面镜子。它的倒影正上前要与它会合，它俩离得越来越近，直到最后……

露珠的恐惧消失了，取而代之的是深深的喜悦，它和广阔的池塘融为了一体。虽然露珠不复存在了，但它并没有毁灭。

它成了整体的一部分。

# The Scenery outside My Window

Anonymous

From the window of my room, I could see a tall cotton-rose hibiscus. In spring, when green foliage was half hidden by mist, the tree looked very enchanting dotted with red blossom. This inspiring neighbour of mine often set my mind working. I gradually regarded it as my best friend.

Nevertheless, when I opened the window one morning, to my amazement, the tree was almost bare beyond recognition as a result of the storm ravages the night before. Struck by the plight, I was seized with a sadness at the thought "all the blossom is doomed to fall". I could not help sighing with emotion: the course of life never runs smooth, for there are so many ups and downs, twists and turns. The vicissitudes of my life saw my beloved friends parting one after another. Isn't it similar to the tree shedding its flowers in the wind?

This event faded from my memory as time went by. One day after I came home from the countryside, I found the room stuffy and casually opened the window. Something outside caught my eye and dazzled me. It was a plum tree all scarlet with blossom

# 窗外的风景

佚名

　　从我房间的窗户向外望去，可以看到一株高大的木芙蓉。春日里，茂密的木芙蓉在薄雾中若隐若现，红花点点，样子实在迷人。它总是赋予我灵感，让我思如泉涌。时间久了，我竟把这木芙蓉视为知己了。

　　然而，有一天清晨，当我推开窗户时，愕然发现前夜的一场风雨已将它摧残得落红满地，丝毫没有了此前迷人的模样。刹那间，一种"花开终有落"的悲凉之感涌上心头。这让我不由得慨叹：在人生这段旅途中，总是少不了种种坎坷，那些曲折起伏的经历才是常态。命运浮沉不定，曾经失去的一个个挚友，不正像这随风而逝的花一般吗？

　　随着时间的流逝，我渐渐地忘却了那天的感触。有一次从乡下回来，觉得屋内的空气有些沉闷，便随手打开了窗户，可就在那一刻，我被眼前的景象惊呆了。窗外有株李子树开花了，满树都是火红的花朵，

set off beautifully by the sunset. The surprise discovery over-whelmed me with pleasure. I wondered why I had no idea of some unyielding life sprouting over the fallen petals when I was grieving for the hibiscus.

When the last withered petal dropped, all the joyful admiration for the hibiscus sank into oblivion as if nothing was left, until the landscape was again ablaze with the red plum blossom to remind people of life's alternation and continuance. Can't it be said that life is actually a symphony, a harmonious composition of loss and gain.

Standing by the window lost in thought for a long time, I realised that no scenery in the world remains unchanged. As long as you keep your heart basking in the sun, every dawn will present a fine prospect for you to unfold and the world will always be about new hopes.

🐟 难词释义 ·················································•

foliage ['fəʊliɪdʒ] *n.* （植物的）枝叶，叶子
ravages ['rævɪdʒɪz] *n.* 破坏；毁坏
plight [plaɪt] *n.* 困境
vicissitude [vɪ'sɪsɪtjuːd] *n.* 变迁；盛衰
oblivion [ə'blɪviən] *n.* 沉睡；遗忘
ablaze [ə'bleɪz] *adj.* 闪耀；发光

在夕阳的映衬下分外美丽。这个意外发现让我惊喜不已。当初自己只顾悲伤，完全没发现在那凄凉景象的背后，另有一番生机正在蓄势萌发。

是啊，当木芙蓉的最后一片花瓣凋落之时，人们以往对它的赞许都成为过眼云烟。可如今，李子树却成长起来了，那火红的花儿正向人们昭示着生命的更迭与繁衍。谁能否认生命原本就是一场得失和谐共存的交响乐呢？

我伫立在窗前沉思良久，是啊，世界上没有一成不变的风景，只要心中向阳，每一个黎明都会向你展现一番美景，这个世界也总会给你带来新的希望。

# Spell of the Rising Moon

Peter Steinhart

There is a hill near my home that I often climb at night. The noise of the city is a far-off murmur. In the hush of dark I share the cheerfulness of crickets and the confidence of owls. But it's the drama of the moonrise that I come to see. For that restores in me a quiet and clarity that the city spends too freely.

From this hill I have watched many moon rise. Each one had its own mood. There have been broad, confident harvest moons in autumn; shy, misty moons in spring; lonely, winter moons rising into the utter silence of an ink-black sky and smoke-smudged orange moons over the dry fields of summer. Each, like fine music, excited my heart and then calmed my soul.

Moon gazing is an ancient art. To prehistoric hunters the moon overhead was as unerring as heartbeat. They knew that every 29 days it became full-bellied and brilliant, then sickened and died, and then was reborn. They knew the waxing moon appeared larger and higher overhead after each succeeding sunset. They knew the waning moon rose later each night until it vanished in the sunrise. To have understood the moon's patterns from experience must have been a profound thing.

# 月出的魅力

[美] 彼得·斯坦哈特

我家附近有座小山，我常去夜爬。在这里，城市的喧嚣都成了遥远的低语。在这黑夜的静谧中，我有幸聆听蟋蟀的欢声和猫头鹰的私语。不过，我上山是来看月出的，因为这可以让我的内心重拾被城市肆意挥霍的宁静与清明。

在这座山上，我欣赏过许多次月亮升起的景象。每一次，月亮的脾性都有所不同。秋天，满月如轮，充满自信；春天，月色迷蒙，看上去羞答答的；冬天，月亮悄无声息地挂在漆黑的夜空中，显得那样孤寂；夏天，橘黄色的月亮似被烟尘笼罩，俯瞰干燥的田野。每一种月景，都像美妙的音乐，使我内心震撼，灵魂平静。

观月是一门古老的艺术。在远古的猎人眼里，天空中月亮变化的规律如同心跳一样准确无误。他们知道每 29 天，月亮就会变得饱满明亮，然后萎缩、消失，而后获得重生。他们知道，月盈期间，每经一次日落，头顶的月亮会显得更高更大；他们还知道，月亏期间，月亮每晚的升起时间都会推迟，待到日出才落。他们竟能根据经验弄清月亮的行踪变化，真是别具慧眼。

But we, who live indoors, have lost contact with the moon. The glare of street lights and the dust of pollution veil the night sky. Though men have walked on the moon, it grows less familiar. Few of us can say what time the moon will rise tonight.

Still, it tugs at our minds. If we unexpectedly encounter the full moon, huge and yellow over the horizon, we are helpless but to stare back at its commanding presence. And the moon has gifts to bestow upon those who watch.

I learned about its gifts one July evening in the mountains. My car had mysteriously stalled, and I was stranded and alone. The sun had set, and I was watching what seems to be the bright-orange glow of a forest fire beyond a ridge to the east. Suddenly, the ridge itself seemed to burst into flame. Then, the rising moon, huge and red and grotesquely misshapen by the dust and sweat of the summer atmosphere, loomed up out of the woods.

Distorted thus by the hot breath of earth, the moon seemed ill-tempered and imperfect. Dogs at nearby farmhouses barked nervously, as if this strange light had wakened evil spirits in the weeds. But as the moon lifted off the ridge it gathered firmness and authority. Its complexion changed from red, to orange, to gold, to impassive yellow. It seemed to draw light out of the darkening earth,

但我们这些深居室内的人已与月亮失去了联系。耀眼的街灯与污浊的烟尘掩盖了夜空。虽然人类已在月球上行走过，但月亮在我们眼中却更加陌生了。很少有人能说出今晚月亮会何时升起。

尽管如此，月亮依然能牵动我们的心。如果我们偶然遇见一轮黄灿灿的硕大满月高高挂在空中，定会禁不住定睛凝望她那高贵的仪容。而月亮也会向那些观赏她的人赐予厚礼。

我是在七月的一个夜晚得到她的厚礼的。当时我正在山上，车突然莫名其妙地熄火了，我孤身一人被困在山中。太阳已经西沉，我看到东边山脊处涌出一团橘黄色的明光，好像森林起火一般。突然，山脊自身似乎也迸射出了火焰。接着，一轮又大又红的月亮从树林里钻了出来，夏天空气中弥漫的灰尘与湿气令它扭曲变形，看上去略显怪异。

月亮被大地灼热的气息扭曲了面目，变得有些暴躁，不再完美如常。附近农舍里的狗不安地狂吠起来，似乎这团奇怪的光亮唤醒了杂草丛中邪恶的幽灵。然而，当月亮缓缓从山脊处升起时，它开始浑身散发着坚定与威严。它的面孔由红色变成橘色，再变成金色，最后变成沉静的黄色。它似乎从黑暗的大地中吸取了光亮，

for as it rose, the hills and valleys below grew dimmer. By the time the moon stood clear of the horizon, full-chested and round and the colour of ivory, the valleys were deep shadows in the landscape. The dogs, reassured that this was the familiar moon, stopped barking. And all at once I felt a confidence and joy close to laughter.

The drama took an hour. Moonrise is slow and serried with subtleties. To watch it, we must slip into an older, more patient sense of time. To watch the moon move inexorably higher is to find an unusual stillness within ourselves. Our imaginations become aware of the vast distances of space, the immensity of the earth and huge improbability of our own existence. We feel small but privileged.

Moonlight shows us none of life's harder edges. Hillsides seem silken and silvery, the oceans still and blue in its light. In moonlight we become less calculating, more drawn to our feelings. And odd things happen in such moments. On that July night, I watched the moon for an hour or two, and then got back into the car, turned the key in the ignition and heard the engine start, just as mysteriously as it had stalled a few hours earlier, I drove down the mountains with the moon on my shoulder and peace in my heart.

因为随着它的升起，下面的山丘和山谷变得越来越暗淡朦胧。等到皓月当空，满月如盘，闪耀着象牙般乳白的清辉时，山谷便成了风景中一片片幽深的阴影。狗确信了那团光是它们熟悉的月亮，也安静下来，停止了吠叫。霎时间，我也觉得信心倍增，心情舒畅，几乎笑出声来。

这奇特的景观持续了一个小时。月出缓慢而微妙。观看月出，我们必须重拾过去那种对时间的耐心。看着月亮势不可挡地一点一点升到空中，会让我们的内心获得一种不同寻常的宁静。我们的想象力让我们看到宇宙的辽阔和大地的广袤，以及我们存在的巨大不可能性。我们甚感渺小，但却深受大自然的厚待。


月色下，我们看不到生活坚硬的棱角。山坡在月光下如同披上了柔和的轻纱，一片银白；大海在月光下显得静谧而碧蓝。我们置身其中，不再像白天那般精于算计，而是任由自己被思绪牵引。这种时候总会发生些怪事。在那个七月的夜晚，我欣赏了一两个小时的月景，然后回到车里，转动钥匙点火，听到引擎启动的声音，就像几个小时前它熄火时那样神秘。我驱车下山回家，身披月光，内心平静。

I return often to the rising moon. I am drawn especially when events crowd ease and clarity of vision into a small corner of my life. This happens often in the fall. Then I go to my hill and await the hunter's moon, enormous and gold over the horizon, filling the night with vision.

An owl swoops from the ridge top, noiseless but bright as flame. A cricket shrills in the grass. I think of poets and musicians. Of Beethoven's *Moonlight Sonata*, and of Shakespeare, whose Lorenzo declaims in *The Merchant of Venice*, "How sweet the moonlight sleeps upon this blank / Here will we sit and let the sounds of music / creep in our ears." I wonder if their verse and music, like the music of crickets are in some way voices of the moon. With such thoughts, my citified confusions melt into the quiet of the night.

Lovers and poets find deeper meaning at night. We are all apt to pose deeper questions about our origins and destinies. We indulge in riddles, rather than in the impersonal geometries that govern the day-lit world. We become philosophers and mystics.

我经常回到山上看月出。尤其是当接踵而来的事情使我身心疲惫、判断失准的时候，我就会对之神往。这种情况通常发生在秋天，然后我就会登上那座小山，等待那轮金黄巨大的猎人之月跃出地平线，为黑夜带来光明。

　　一只猫头鹰从山顶俯冲下来，无声无息，犹如一道火焰闪过。蟋蟀在草丛中高歌。我想到了诗人和音乐家，想起了贝多芬的《月光奏鸣曲》，以及莎士比亚笔下《威尼斯商人》中洛伦佐的话："月光沉睡在这岸边多么甜美！／我们坐在这里，让音乐之声／潜入我们的耳内。"我不知道他们的诗句和乐曲是否像蟋蟀的歌声一样，都可算作月亮的微语。想到这些，我那被喧嚣的城市扰乱了的心绪也融化在了夜的幽静之中。

　　在夜里，恋人和诗人往往能找到生活更深刻的意义，我们也倾向于问一些关于生命起源和命运走向的深刻问题。在夜里，我们沉溺于难解的谜团，而不是那些统治着白昼世界的刻板理论。在夜里，我们都成了哲学家和神秘主义者。

At moonrise, as we slow our minds to the pace of the heavens, enchantment steals over us. We open the vents of feeling and exercise parts of our minds that reason locks away by day. We hear, across the distances, murmurs of ancient hunters and see anew the visions of poets and lovers of long ago.

🐟 难词释义 ·········································································· •

hush [hʌʃ] *n.* 寂静，鸦雀无声

unerring [ʌn'ɜːrɪŋ] *adj.* 一贯正确的

tug [tʌg] *v.* （用力地）拉，拖，拽

stall [stɔːl] *v.* （使）熄火，抛锚

strand [strænd] *v.* 使滞留，使困在（某处）

grotesquely [grəʊ'teskli] *adv.* 奇异地；荒诞地

serried ['serid] *adj.* 密集的

ignition [ɪg'nɪʃn] *n.* 点火装置

swoop [swuːp] *v.* 俯冲；（尤指鸟）猛扑

vent [vent] *n.* （强烈情绪或能量的）发泄，表达

月出之时，当我们放慢思绪，让它与天国的节奏同步，一种心醉神迷的感觉会流遍全身。我们打开情感的窗口，让白天被理智锁住的那部分思绪尽情奔涌。我们穿越时空，聆听远古猎人的低语，重新看到许久以前诗人与恋人眼中的景象。

彼得·斯坦哈特（Peter Steinhart，1943—）

美国自然主义作家、艺术家，曾连续 12 年担任美国《奥杜邦杂志》专栏作家，还曾两次入围美国国家杂志奖。他的散文优美清新，给人以美的享受。

# Whistling of Birds (Excerpts)

David Herbert Lawrence

The frost held for many weeks, until the birds were dying rapidly. Everywhere in the fields and under the hedges lay the ragged remains of lapwings, starlings, thrushes, innumerable ragged bloody cloaks of birds, when the flesh was eaten by invisible beasts of prey.

Then, quite suddenly, one morning, the change came. The wind went to the south, came off the sea warm and soothing. In the afternoon there were little gleams of sunshine, and the doves began, without interval, slowly and awkwardly to coo. The doves were cooing, though with a laboured sound, as if they were still winter-stunned. ...Then, in the yellow-gleamy sunset, wild birds began to whistle faintly in the blackthorn thickets of the streambottom.

...How could they sing at once, when the ground was thickly strewn with the torn carcasses of birds? Yet out of the evening came the uncertain, silvery sounds that made one's soul start alert, almost with fear. How could the little silver bugles sound the rally so swiftly, in the soft air, when the earth was yet bound?

# 鸟啼（节选）

[英] 戴维·赫伯特·劳伦斯 | 于晓丹 译

严寒持续了好几个星期，鸟儿大批地死去。田间与灌木篱下，横陈着田凫、椋鸟、画眉等数不清的腐鸟的血衣，鸟儿的肉身已被隐秘的老饕吃净了。

突然间，一个清晨，变化出现了。风刮向南方，海上飘来了温暖和慰藉。午后，太阳露出了几星光亮，鸽子开始不停歇地咕咕叫，缓慢而笨拙。这声音显得有些吃力，仿佛还没有从严冬的打击下缓过来。……夕阳西下时，从河床上的黑刺李丛中，开始传出野鸟微弱的啼鸣。

……地上还都是被撕碎的鸟的尸体，它们怎么会突然歌唱起来？从夜色中浮起的声音隐约而清越，令人灵魂一颤，甚是胆寒。当大地仍封冻之时，那小小的清越之声已经在柔软的空气中吹响呼唤春天的号角了。

Yet the birds continued their whistling, rather dimly and brokenly, but throwing the threads of silver, germinating noise into the air.

...

There is another world. The winter is gone. There is a new world of spring. The voice of the turtle is heard in the land. In the bottoms of impenetrable blackthorn, each evening and morning now, out flickers a whistling of birds. Where does it come from, the song? After so long a cruelty, how can they make it up so quickly?

All the time, whilst the earth lay choked and killed and winter-mortified, the deep undersprings were quiet. They only wait for the ponderous encumbrance of the old order to give way, yield in the thaw, and there they are, a silver realm at once. Under the surge of ruin, unmitigated winter, lies the silver potentiality of all blossom. One day the black tide must spend itself and fade back. Then all-suddenly appears the crocus, hovering triumphant in the rear, and we know the order has changed, there is a new regime.

Even whilst we stare at the ragged horror of birds scattered broadcast, part-eaten, the soft, uneven cooing of the pigeon ripples from the outhouses, and there is a faint silver whistling in the bushes come twilight.

它们的啼鸣，虽然含糊，若断若续，却把明快而萌发的声音抛向苍穹。

......

世界更迭了。冬去春来，全新的世界开启了。田地间响起斑鸠的叫声。在无法穿越的黑刺李丛中，每天早晚都会传出鸟儿的啼鸣。这歌声到底来自何处？刚经历过一段漫长的残酷时期，鸟儿怎么会这么快就重整旗鼓？

当大地因寒冬受困、冰封之时，深埋在地心深处的春日生机始终一片寂默，只等着旧秩序的重荷让位退去。冰消雪化之后，顷刻间现出银光闪烁的王国。在毁灭一切的寒冬巨浪之下，蛰伏着令所有鲜花盛开的琼浆。总有一天，那黑暗的潮水会耗尽消退，番红花显现在潮尾，胜利地摇曳。于是我们知道，规律变了，这是一片新的天地。

即使当我们凝视着遍野横陈的鸟尸残骸时，屋外也会传来鸽子此起彼伏的咕咕声，灌木丛中也会传出鸟儿微弱的啼鸣。

No matter, we stand and stare at the torn and unsightly ruins of life, we watch the weary, mutilated columns of winter retreating under our eyes. Yet in our ears are the silver bugles of a new creation advancing on us from behind, we hear the rolling of the soft and happy drums of the doves.

We may not choose the world. We have hardly any choice for ourselves. We follow with our eyes the bloody and horrid line of march of this extreme winter, as it passes away. But we cannot hold back the spring. We cannot make the birds silent, prevent the bubbling of wood-pigeons. We cannot stay the fine world of silver-fecund creation from gathering itself and taking place upon us. Whether we will or not, the daphne tree will soon be giving off perfume, the lambs dancing on two feet, the celandines will twinkle all over the ground, there will be a new heaven and new earth.

...

不管怎样，我们站在那里，凝视着惨不忍睹的生命毁灭景象，疲惫的残冬在我们眼皮底下撤退了。我们耳中充塞的，是新生的造物清明而生动的号音。那造物从身后赶来，我们听到了鸽子奏出的轻柔而欢快的隆隆鼓声。

或许我们无法选择世界。我们也很少能进行自主选择。我们只能用眼睛跟随极端的寒冬那沾满血迹的骇人行列，直至其过去。但是我们无法阻挡春天，无法令鸟儿沉寂，无法阻止林鸽咕咕叫，不能滞留美好世界中丰饶的创造，它们不可阻挡地振作自己，来到我们身边。不管我们情愿与否，月桂树很快就会散发出芬芳，羔羊很快就要站立舞蹈，燕子草会遍地闪烁点点光亮，那将是一个崭新的天地。

……

Such a long, long winter, and the frost only broke yesterday. Yet it seems, already, we cannot remember it. It is strange, the utter incompatibility of death with life. Whilst there is death, life is not to be found. It is all death, one overwhelming flood. And then a new tide rises, and it is all life, a fountain of silvery blissfulness...

🐬 难词释义

hedge [hedʒ] *n.* 树篱

lapwing ['læpwɪŋ] *n.* 田凫

starling ['stɑːlɪŋ] *n.* 椋鸟

thrush [θrʌʃ] *n.* 画眉

blackthorn ['blækθɔːn] *n.* 黑刺李（李树的一种）

strew [struː] *v.* 在……上布满（或散播）

carcass ['kɑːkəs] *n.* 动物尸体

bugle ['bjuːgl] *n.* 喇叭；军号

germinate ['dʒɜːmɪneɪt] *v.* （使）发芽，萌芽

ponderous ['pɒndərəs] *adj.* 笨重的

encumbrance [ɪn'kʌmbrəns] *n.* 累赘；妨碍物

thaw [θɔː] *n.* 解冻时期，融化季节

unmitigated [ʌn'mɪtɪgeɪtɪd] *adj.* 十足的，彻底的

crocus ['krəʊkəs] *n.* 番红花

ripple ['rɪpl] *v.* 扩散

mutilate ['mjuːtɪleɪt] *v.* 毁坏；使伤残

celandine ['seləndaɪn] *n.* 燕子草

多么漫长的冬天，冰封昨天才裂开。但看上去，我们已把它全然忘记了。真奇怪，生命和死亡全不相容。死时，生便不存在，皆是死亡，犹如洪水般势不可挡。继而，一股新的浪头涌起，便又全是生命，化成银色的极乐源泉汩汩向前……

戴维·赫伯特·劳伦斯（David Herbert Lawrence，1885—1930）

英国诗人、小说家、散文家。其作品提倡人性自由发展，反对工业文明对自然的破坏，对家庭、婚姻和性进行了深入探索，对 20 世纪的小说写作产生了广泛影响。代表作有《查泰莱夫人的情人》《儿子与情人》《虹》《恋爱中的女人》等。

本书中有一些篇目的作者或译者暂未能联系上，敬请各位与我们联系，以便支付稿费。期盼广大读者对本书提出宝贵意见，我们将不断修订，使本书趋于完善。

联系方式：dyts@xdf.cn

人的一生恰如一首诗，
自有其韵律和节奏。

图书在版编目（CIP）数据

向阳而生：抚愈心灵的经典英语美文 / 周成刚主编. — 北京：世界图书出版
有限公司北京分公司, 2024.1
ISBN 978-7-5232-0957-8

Ⅰ. ①向… Ⅱ. ①周… Ⅲ. ①英语－语言读物 Ⅳ. ①H319.4

中国国家版本馆CIP数据核字(2023)第223416号

| 书　　名 | 向阳而生：抚愈心灵的经典英语美文 |
| | XIANGYANG ER SHENG |
| 主　　编 | 周成刚 |
| 责任编辑 | 梁沁宁 |
| 封面设计 | 申海风 |
| 版式设计 | 申海风 |
| 文字编辑 | 刘婷婷 |
| 插画设计 | 欧永陆 |
| 出版发行 | 世界图书出版有限公司北京分公司 |
| 地　　址 | 北京市东城区朝内大街 137 号 |
| 邮　　编 | 100010 |
| 电　　话 | 010-64038355（发行）　64033507（总编室） |
| 网　　址 | http://www.wpcbj.com.cn |
| 邮　　箱 | wpcbjst@vip.163.com |
| 销　　售 | 新华书店 |
| 印　　刷 | 北京盛通印刷股份有限公司 |
| 开　　本 | 880mm×1230mm　1/32 |
| 印　　张 | 8.5 |
| 字　　数 | 142 千字 |
| 版　　次 | 2024 年 1 月第 1 版 |
| 印　　次 | 2024 年 1 月第 1 次印刷 |
| 国际书号 | ISBN 978-7-5232-0957-8 |
| 定　　价 | 68.00 元 |